T0329539

The Risk Premium Factor

Founded in 1807, John Wiley & Sons is the oldest independent publishing company in the United States. With offices in North America, Europe, Australia and Asia, Wiley is globally committed to developing and marketing print and electronic products and services for our customers' professional and personal knowledge and understanding.

The Wiley Finance series contains books written specifically for finance and investment professionals as well as sophisticated individual investors and their financial advisors. Book topics range from portfolio management to e-commerce, risk management, financial engineering, valuation and financial instrument analysis, as well as much more.

For a list of available titles, please visit our Web site at www.WileyFinance.com.

The Risk Premium Factor

A New Model for Understanding the Volatile Forces that Drive Stock Prices

STEPHEN D. HASSETT

WILEY

John Wiley & Sons, Inc.

Published by John Wiley & Sons, Inc., Hoboken, New Jersey.
Published simultaneously in Canada.

For general information on our other products and services or for technical support, please contact our Customer Care Department within the United States at (800) 762-2974, outside the United States at (317) 572-3993 or fax (317) 572-4002.

Wiley also publishes its books in a variety of electronic formats. Some content that appears in print may not be available in electronic books. For more information about Wiley products, visit our web site at www.wiley.com.

Library of Congress Cataloging-in-Publication Data:

Hassett, Stephen D., 1961–
 The risk premium factor: a new model for understanding the volatile forces that drive stock prices / Stephen D. Hassett.
     p. cm. — (Wiley finance series ; 702)
   Includes index.
   ISBN 978-1-118-09905-6 (cloth); ISBN 9781118118597 (ebk);
   ISBN 9781118118603 (ebk); ISBN 9781118118610 (ebk)
  1. Stocks–Prices.   2. Corporations–Valuation.   3. Business cycles.   4. Stock exchanges.
 I. Title.
   HG4551.H34 2011
   332.63′222—dc23
                                                                        2011017550

10   9   8   7   6   5   4   3   2   1

To Anne, Sarah, and Charlotte Hassett

Contents

List of Figures

List of Tables

Meet Charlie, just your typical office worker, who spent many years getting beaten down in his office football pool. Each week he'd put in his $10, and each week he'd lose. Charlie loved football and was always supremely confident in his picks; he just couldn't pick against the spread.

One day, Charlie was home looking over the coming week's games. His young daughter asked what he was doing. He explained. Then, thinking about his poor track record, he asked his daughter if she'd like to help. She was thrilled.

"Eagles at Cowboys—who do you like?" he said.

"Eagles," she said.

"Why?" asked Charlie.

"Eagles are pretty," said his daughter.

"Dolphins at Jets?"

She responded, "Dolphins, they're cute."

And on it went.

By Sunday night, Charlie had 10 wins and 2 losses. He won again on Monday for his best week ever. Charlie won again that week, and the next. Whenever someone asked Charlie what his new secret was, Charlie would say, "I have a system." If pressed, Charlie would even give detailed ex-post analysis to support his picks.

Then Charlie lost, and kept losing.

While Charlie claimed expertise and a system, really he just had a run of good luck. If anyone asked Charlie to explain why his real system worked, he couldn't. This is obviously a parable for investing.

Like Charlie's daughter, investors will often try to justify their gut feel decisions with some explanation. Unfortunately, these explanations can be misleading or confusing. You can read Malcolm Gladwell's *Blink* (Little, Brown, 2005) or Jonah Lehrer's *How We Decide* (Houghton Mifflin Harcourt, 2009) to get a full appreciation of our flawed ability to develop explanations that justify our gut feelings. The average investor is bombarded with conflicting and confusing messages on television and in print. Not only can these reinforce the flawed rationalization, but they can be based on flawed attempts at developing an explanation themselves. To make matters worse, the average investor also runs American business, so this confusion extends to day-to-day decision making, where executives often make decisions to please the market. Whether you are investing as a corporate decision maker, private equity investor, venture capitalist, or individual investor, if you don't understand how the market values businesses, you really don't understand your system. Having a good investment track record does not mean you understand value; it may just mean you are lucky.

Professors Eugene F. Fama and Kenneth French compared risk-adjusted returns of actively managed mutual funds to what would be expected to happen by chance. After running 10,000 simulations, they found that the actual performance distributions were about the same as for the simulations. Not only were the differences in mutual fund performance consistent with what you would expect to find by chance, but when fees were included, actively managed mutual funds *underperformed* the market.[1]

Many others have similar findings. A study by Standard & Poor's found that fund managers tend to not outperform consistently:

> *Over the five years ending September 2009, only 4.27% large-cap funds, 3.98% mid-cap funds, and 9.13% small-cap funds maintained a top-half ranking over the five consecutive 12-month periods. No large- or mid-cap funds, and only one small-cap fund maintained a top quartile ranking over the same period.*[2]

While understanding value does not assure success, it improves your odds and is an important component in successful investing. Since investing is about maximizing value, with every decision, you should be asking, "Am I creating value?" The good news is that understanding value and the things that drive value are not complicated. It's about just three things: earnings, interest rates, and long-term growth.

EVOLUTION OF A THEORY

I began formulating my theory in 1998, while I was with Stern Stewart & Co., a management consulting firm in New York. I began questioning the arguments in the financial press that the equity markets were overvalued based on high price-to-earnings (P/E) ratios with no discussion of how interest rates impacted valuation. Through my years of corporate development where I valued numerous acquisitions, and my corporate financial strategy work with Stern Stewart, I knew that the cost of equity was a key driver in valuation where higher cost of equity results in lower valuations.

This book sets a foundation, then walks through the simple process of understanding value. It begins with some theory that led to a discovery. I will summarize it here. Don't be intimidated if you don't follow it all yet, we will revisit it step by step in the first part of this book.

A risk premium, in general, is the amount of excess return an investor expects for taking on risk, and the equity risk premium is the amount of risk that investors expect above a riskless investment, like Treasury bonds, for investing in the stock market. Many, if not most, theorists assumed the equity risk premium was a constant based on historical premiums above the risk-free rate.

I began hypothesizing that that the equity risk premium is not a static number but a variable that fluctuates in direct proportion to the long-term risk-free rate. The central idea is that the risk premium is fixed as a percentage of the risk-free rate, not a fixed premium. Intuitively, this seems to make sense, but I needed to prove it. Using a constant growth equation, I made some simplifying assumptions and ran the numbers, and it seemed to work.

But if it were so simple, why had no one else thought of it? Admittedly, this question caused me to pause—for more than 10 years. I periodically updated my theory over the next decade and was glad to see it all still worked, and wondered: why don't people know how simple the market really is? I can't answer these two questions, but I do know that misperceptions about the stock market are a serious problem. They cause individuals, companies, and even governments to make bad decisions and bad investments. Perhaps the most significant is the lack of understanding among many corporate executives of how their strategic and tactical decisions translate to valuation.

I finally published my new theory in the *Journal of Applied Corporate Finance* in early 2010.[3] This book expands on that article, introduces new concepts and applications, and updates the results of the model through early 2011.

OVERVIEW

Understanding the stock market requires a little math, but nothing more than addition, subtraction, multiplication, and division. This book introduces a simple formula based on readily available data that has explained market cycles for the past 50 years. By understanding how investors value the stock market, executives can apply the same simple concepts to corporate decisions to increase value.

Above all, this book is about dispelling the notions that the stock market is a mysterious arbiter of value, when, in fact, it is easy to understand and almost reptilian in response to readily observable factors. Reptiles respond in very predictable and instinctive ways using their small brains. Surprisingly, so does the market, and it's all linked to some deep-rooted psychological behavior called *loss aversion* uncovered by Daniel Kahneman and Amos Tversky in the late 1970s (Kahneman won the Nobel Prize). This book exposes the stock market's small brain and introduces a very simple (small-brain) model that shows that the market responds to just three factors: earnings, long-term growth, and interest rates.

If you are not a numbers person, I have some bad news; if you want to understand the stock market, you need to do some math. The good news is that all you really need is addition, subtraction, multiplication, and division. If you can do that, you can understand the stock market because the value of the market can be expressed with a very simple formula. For the numbers people, I will show how the formulas and assumptions are derived along with exploring advanced decision-making applications. Non-numbers people, don't be intimidated. When I present a formula, it will be preceded or followed by a description of the inputs or variables. Read them. They are not complicated.

This book also links stock market value to corporate decision making. While the theoretical linkage has always been there, understanding and belief have largely been absent. By understanding *and believing* basic valuation concepts, decision makers will be in a better decision to make value-creating decisions. If you are already a sophisticated investor or financial analyst, you are undoubtedly very familiar with many of the concepts and arguments discussed in this book. You will be in the best position to appreciate the simplicity with which old and new concepts are combined to produce a new way of understanding value in the market.

Understanding the factors that drive the stock market is more than an academic exercise. With a framework to understanding what drives the overall market, business leaders are positioned to drive value in their own businesses. While driving increases in shareholder value is one of the most important responsibilities of any business leader, many are handicapped by not having a deep understanding of the true drivers of value. Others are handicapped because they simply don't believe that the market actually behaves in a way that is consistent with the theories they have been taught. They are not alone. Even prominent economists claim stock market valuation is not fully understood. In a 1984 speech to the American Finance Association, Lawrence Summers said:

> *It would surely come as a surprise to a layman to learn that virtually no mainstream research in the field of finance in the past decade has attempted to account for the stock-market boom of the 1960s or the spectacular decline in real stock prices during the mid-1970s.*[4]

Some people see the stock market as arbitrary and random in setting values. But despite occasional bouts of extreme volatility (including, of course, the recent crash), most academics (and many practitioners) would likely agree with the proposition that the market does a reasonably good job of incorporating available information in share prices. At the same time, however, certain factors can clearly cause the market to misprice assets. These include problems with liquidity, imperfect information, and unrealistic expectations that can knock valuations out of line for a period of time. But such limitations notwithstanding, over a longer horizon the market appears to be reasonably efficient in correcting these aberrations. The valuation model introduced in this book explains market value and helps identify periods where mispricing may be evident.

This book introduces a model called the Risk Premium Factor (RPF) Valuation Model. The RPF Model explains the stock market and provides a quantitative explanation for the booms, busts, bubbles, multiple expansion, and contractions we have experienced over the past 50 years. The model explains stock prices from 1960 through February 2011, (the time of this writing) including the 2008–2009 "market meltdown." It does this with a new and original, but surprisingly simple, approach that combines generally accepted approaches to valuation with a new way of estimating the market or equity risk premium (ERP) that produces very good explanations of market P/E ratios and overall market levels. Figures P.1 and P.2 show how the P/E predicted by the model, when applied to S&P operating earnings, explains levels of the S&P 500 since 1986 on a monthly basis over the past 50 years on an annual basis.

My approach to estimating the ERP (discussed in detail later) is the most original part of this overall hypothesis. Many, if not most, theorists assumed the ERP was a constant based on historical premiums above the risk-free rate (generally 10-year or 30-year Treasury yields). If we assume that long-term real interest rates do not fluctuate and real growth can be approximated by real long-term gross domestic product (GDP) growth that is also generally assumed to be stable, the market-wide P/E would always be a constant if the risk premium is also fixed. But, of course, the P/E multiple on the earnings of the S&P 500 is volatile, with year-end values ranging from 7.3 in 1974 to 29.5 in 2001.

A constant risk premium implies that investors are satisfied with a proportionately smaller premium as the risk free rate increases. I suggest that the ERP is not a static number but a variable that fluctuates in direct proportion to the long-term risk-free rate as a fixed percentage, not a fixed premium. In other words, the premium maintains constant relative rather than absolute relationship. With this new insight, the risk premium can be determined by

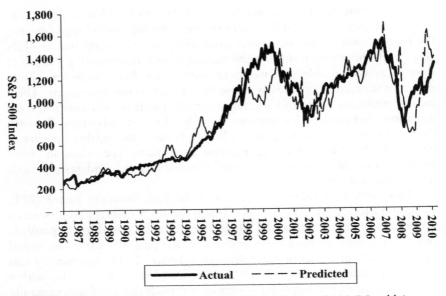

FIGURE P.1 S&P 500 Actual vs. Predicted, 1986–February 2011 (Monthly)
Source: S&P earnings and price from 1988 to Present, from Standard & Poor's web site (www.standardandpoors.com/indices/sp-500/en/us/?indexId=spusa-500-usduf–p–us–l–); S&P monthly earnings for 1/86–11/88 from "Online Data Robert Shiller" (www.econ.yale.edu/-shiller/data.htm); treasury yields from Federal Reserve, H.15 Selected Interest Rates (www.federalreserve.gov/datadownload/Choose.aspx?rel=H.15). Since earnings are released quarterly, the model was extended to monthly and daily price data by using operating earnings as a constant for each month in the quarter applied for the month preceding quarter end (i.e., December to February = Q1) under the assumption that market expectations would have incorporated earning expectations. Calculations and methodology by the author.

the following formula:

$$\text{Equity Risk Premium} = \text{Risk Free Long-Term Rate}$$

$$\times \text{Risk Premium Factor (1.48)}$$

This also explains why the risk premium varies over time; as interest rates vary, so does the risk premium. This risk premium factor (RPF) seems to hold steady for long periods of time, changing just twice from 1960 to present (February 2011). The RPF was 1.24 from 1960 to 1980, 0.90 from 1981 to June 2002, and 1.48 from July 2002 to the present. As shown in

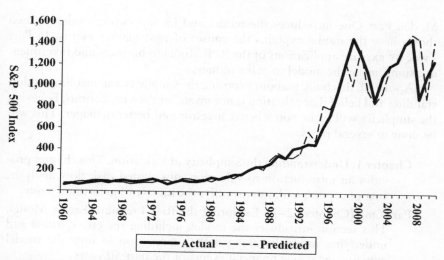

FIGURE P.2   S&P 500 Actual vs. Predicted, 1960–2010
Source: S&P earnings and price from 1988 to present from Standard & Poor's web
site (www.standardandpoors.com/indices/sp-500/en/us/?indexId=spusa-500-
usduf–p-us-l–); S&P averages 1960 to 1988 from Damodaran Online: Home Page
for Answath Damodaran (New York University) (http://pages.stern.nyu.edu/
~adamodar/); Treasury yields from Federal Reserve, H.15 Selected Interest Rates
(www.federalreserve.gov/datadownload/Choose.aspx?rel=H.15). Calculations and
methodology by the author.

Figure P.2, the model does a very good job of predicting market levels, even
through the present financial crisis.

This result is also consistent with "loss aversion," the well-documented
(by Kahneman and Tversky) willingness of investors to sacrifice significant
gains to avoid considerably smaller losses. In one study, they found that
the coefficient was 2.25.[5] This implies that on average, participants would
be indifferent to a coin flip to win $225 or lose $100. This is the same
as choosing between a guaranteed $100 versus a coin flip for $325.[6] The
analogous calculation for the RPF model would suggest that if the risk-free
rate is 4 percent and the RPF is 1.48, a $1,000 investment bond would offer
a guaranteed $40, and equities a required return of $99.

HOW THIS BOOK IS STRUCTURED

All of these concepts will be explored in detail. Chapter 1 reviews the basics
of valuation, setting the stage for Part One, the introduction of the RPF

Model. Part One introduces the model and its supporting evidence, then shows how the model explains the causes of past market events. In Part Two, we explore applications of the RPF Model to business and investment decisions, using the model to make money.

Above all, this book is about exposing the simplicity and instilling understanding and belief that valuation is not mystic or even mysterious. Believing the simplicity will make you a better investor and better manager. This will be done in several parts:

Chapter 1: Understanding the Simplicity of Valuation. This chapter provides an introduction to valuation, discounted cash flow analysis, cost of capital, and, importantly, the impact of growth on value.

Part One (Chapters 2–4): Exploring the Risk Premium Factor Model. This section introduces the model, including the effectiveness and underlying rationale, along with a discussion of how the model explains the major financial events of the past 50 years.

Part Two (Chapters 5–11): Applying the Risk Premium Factor Valuation Model. This section reviews a variety of applications of the model, including valuation for mergers and acquisitions, new ventures, stock market, and growth rates implied by stock price.

The companion web site for this book includes data, tools, and links to additional reading and resources.

AS YOU BEGIN

This book dispels the notions that the stock market is a mysterious arbiter of value, when, in fact, it is easy to understand and almost reptilian in response to readily observable factors. It is designed to remove the mystery, to help make you a better investor and better manager.

STEPHEN D. HASSETT

Acknowledgments

I first want to thank my wife, Anne, for her patience and critical eye in helping me develop and especially edit this book. I also want to thank those who provided important feedback as I evolved this work from theory to working paper to article to book.

It starts with Bob Bruner, who is now dean of the Darden Graduate School of Business Administration at the University of Virginia, who was my finance professor. His incredibly engaging case method teaching of finance sparked my initial interest in mergers and acquisitions that eventually led to this book. Back in 2006, he also took the time review my initial few pages of notes, formulas and charts, and encouraged me to pursue my research. Bob referred me to Ken Eades, also at Darden, who was very generous with his time and offered me early encouragement and feedback as I moved my research from notes to working paper to article.

Don Chew, editor of the *Journal of Applied Corporate Finance* (owned by Morgan Stanley and published by Wiley), not only published my article, but provided editing that made my original work so much better. John McCormack, associate editor of the *Journal of Applied Corporate Finance*, provided important critical feedback and suggestions as I developed my JACF article—all of which is now reflected in this book.

Roger Grabowski at Duff & Phelps, and coauthor of *Cost of Capital: Applications and Examples* (Wiley, 2010) took an interest in my work after reading the JACF article and subsequently provided great feedback and new ideas for expanding some of my original applications.

Finally, I would like to thank my agent, Bob Diforio, who took a chance on a first-time author, as well as the team at Wiley who patiently guided me through the publication process while improving the finished product: Debra Englander, Editorial Director, Emilie Herman, Senior Editorial Manager, and Donna Martone, Senior Production Editor.

S. D. H.

About the Author

Stephen D. Hassett is a corporate development executive with Sage North America, a subsidiary of The Sage Group plc, a leading global supplier of business management software and services. He published "The Risk Premium Factor Valuation Model for Calculating the Equity Market Risk Premium and Explaining the Value of the S&P with Two Variables" in the *Journal of Applied Corporate Finance* (Spring 2010) and is a regular contributing author for the Seeking Alpha investment web site.

Hassett was previously Vice President, International and Emerging Businesses (New Ventures), for the Weather Channel Interactive, where he started a successful merger-and-acquisition program. He oversaw new growth opportunities and businesses, including Web and mobile properties in Europe, Asia, Latin America. Prior to joining the Weather Channel, Hassett was with Servidyne, Inc., which acquired iTendant, a SaaS software company where he was CEO and cofounder. Previously, he was with Stern Stewart & Co., a management consulting firm specializing in value-based management, where he was a vice president, advising clients and leading engagements to increase shareholder value through corporate and financial strategy, value-based management, mergers and acquisitions, and the design and implementation of Stern Stewart's proprietary EVA® framework for decision making and incentives in a variety of industries, including media, technology, and manufacturing. Prior to that, Hassett was Vice President, Development of the Architectural Products Group of Oldcastle, Inc., a Global 500 company, where he was responsible for merger-and-acquisitions, strategy, and planning. Earlier in his career, Hassett was a systems consultant with Watson Wyatt, where he designed and programmed PC and mainframe systems.

He holds an MBA from the Darden Graduate School of Business Administration at the University of Virginia and a BS in management systems from Rensselaer Polytechnic Institute.[*]

---

[*]The opinions expressed in this book are mine and do not necessarily reflect those of any past or present employers or clients.

Understanding the Simplicity of Valuation

The constant growth equation is a simple model for valuing a stream of cash flows in perpetuity based on cost of capital and long-term growth. By using earnings as a proxy for cash flow, this simple model can estimate fair value of the stock market. Understanding how lower cost of capital and higher growth rates translate to higher price-to-earnings (P/E) ratios, thus higher valuation, and that even small changes make a big difference is one of the most important lessons from the Risk Premium Factor (RPF) Model. The Capital Asset Pricing Model (CAPM) is used to determine cost of equity capital where the equity risk premium (ERP) is a key component. Despite its importance in valuation, most methods for estimating the ERP have been unsatisfactory.

Understanding the drivers of value requires familiarity with a few basic financial concepts. The first is the *time value of money*. This term refers to the idea that money promised at some future date is less valuable than money in hand today. Would you rather have $100 today or in one year? Of course, you'd rather have the $100 today to spend, invest, or pay down debt. At a 5 percent annual interest rate, $100 invested today is worth $105 in a year. We call this the *future value* (FV).

Conversely, assuming the same rate of return, $105 in a year is worth $100 today. This is referred to as *discounted value*. Discounting a stream of cash flows over several periods is discounted cash flow (DCF) analysis. This discount rate is the amount by which we discount future payments or cash flow to find their equivalent value today. It is also called the *cost of capital*—a term that will be used throughout this book and abbreviated by "C."

How much is the promise to pay $100 in a year with C of 5 percent worth today? We call this the present value (PV). If you think it is $95, you are close, but wrong. A simple test is to take the estimated PV and use the discount rate to get the FV. In this case, if you invested $95 at 5 percent, you would have only $99.75 at the end of a year. In order to calculate present value, you need to divide by the discount rate (C). The math is simple. The future value in one year equals the present value (our original amount) plus the present value times the interest rate. Think of it this way, if you deposit $100 (PV) in the bank at 5 percent (C) at the end of one year, you have your initial $100 plus $100 times 5 percent.

FV = PV + PV × C, which is usually simplified to:

$$FV = PV \times (1 + C)$$

In our first example, that would be:

$$\$105 = \$100 \times (1 + 0.05)$$

Therefore, we can just rearrange the equation to solve for PV:
FV/(1 + C) = PV, so to find the future value of $100 at 5 percent:

$$\$100/(1 + 0.05) = \$95.24$$

In other words, $95.24 invested for one year at 5 percent is $100.

Next, let's look at values over longer periods. What is the value of $100 at 5% in five years with interest paid at the end of each year and reinvested? At the end of year one, we have $105. The $105 is reinvested at 5 percent to return $110.25 at the end of year 2. At the end of year 3, $115.76. And at the end of year 5, $127.63. This is simply taking the PV and multiplying by (1 + C) once for each year.

This can also be expressed as:

$$FV = PV \times (1 + C)^n \text{ where } n \text{ represents the number of years.}$$

In our example, that is:

$$\$127.63 = \$100 \times (1.05)^5$$

This is another way of saying we multiply by 1.05, five times. The formula for PV is:

$$PV = FV/(1 + C)^n$$

In words, we just divide by 1 + C once for each year.

RATES, COMPOUNDING, AND TIME VALUE

Interest rates have an obvious impact on time value. If instead of 5 percent you were able to invest at 10 percent per year, your annual return doubles. One hundred dollars at 10 percent is worth $110 in a year and $121 in two years. At the end of five years it is worth $161, compared to $127 at 5 percent. The calculation of reinvested interest plus principal over a number of years is called compounding. The compounding of interest results in ever growing returns over time with the impact of interest rates magnifying over time. While the difference between 5 percent and 10 percent for a year might not seem like much, over five years the initial investment would have grown just 27 percent at 5 percent, while growing 61 percent at a 10 percent annual rate. After 10 years at 5 percent the original $100 will have grown to just $163, while the investment of $100 at 10 percent will have grown to $259. Just as future value increases with the discount rate, present value decreases. The present value of $100 paid in five years at 5 percent is $78.35, while the present value at 10% is just $62.09. The higher the discount rate, the less that future dollar is worth.

We can see this in the equations. Since $FV = PV \times (1 + C)^n$, the larger the discount rate (C) and the longer it is invested in years (n), the more it grows. The opposite holds true for PV, since the equation for $PV = FV/(1 + C)^n$, as C or n gets larger, the PV gets smaller. I am spending a lot of time on this point because, as we will see, the cost of capital (C) has a big influence on stock price.

WHY TIME VALUE MATTERS FOR THE STOCK MARKET

When you buy stock in a company, you are buying ownership. Just as an owner of 100 percent of a business owns 100 percent of the future cash flow, an owner of 0.01 percent of a company, owns 0.01 percent of its future cash flow. It is that cash flow that accounts for the value. If you own 100 percent of a business, you decide how that cash flow is invested—pay dividends or reinvest. If you own only a small part of the business—like a typical shareholder—you are entrusting management to decide how to dispose of its cash flow. They can pay dividends, reinvest, buy back shares, or acquire another business.

If we forecast future cash flows of a business, projecting out all revenue, expenses, and investment, the value of the business is equal to the present value of those cash flows. Valuation of companies reflects current earnings and future earnings—growth; but the more distant the earnings, the less value today.

How far in the future do we discount the earnings? In perpetuity—in other words, forever. Of course, the company could be sold in the next few years, but since the sale price is based on projected cash flow, the valuation at time of sale will still be based on perpetuity cash flows. As you will see, projecting future earnings into perpetuity does not require a spreadsheet with an infinite number of columns.

VALUING A PERPETUITY

If I promise to pay you $5 per year forever, what is that worth today? If we assume C is still 5 percent, then the payment at the end of the first year is worth $5/(1 + 0.05) and the second $5/(1 + 0.05)^2 and so on. Table 1.1 shows the discount factors and present value for select future years. The PV in any year is the payment divided by the discount factor. The PV of the perpetuity is the sum of the PVs for each year out to infinity.

The good news is that in order to calculate a perpetuity, you don't need to forecast cash flows forever. Assuming a constant discount rate and cash flow the value of a perpetuity is simply:

$$PV = E/C,$$

where E is the annual cash flow in each year. Notice that since E is divided by C, PV gets larger as C gets smaller—lower interest rates make values go up. Since in evaluating a company, E is not a constant we need to account for its growth.

TABLE 1.1 PV of $5 at 5 Percent

Year	Discount Factor	PV
1	1.050	$4.76
2	1.103	$4.54
3	1.158	$4.32
4	1.216	$4.11
5	1.276	$3.92
10	1.629	$3.07
100	131.501	$0.04

CONSTANT GROWTH EQUATION: THE KEY TO UNDERSTANDING THE STOCK MARKET

Transforming the perpetuity equation to account for growth only requires subtracting the long-term growth rate (G) from C in the perpetuity formula, so PV = E/C becomes:

$$PV = E/(C - G)$$

Notice again that since you are dividing E by C – G, as G increases, so does PV. This makes intuitive sense. If you are starting with the same cash flow (E) and discount rate (C), then obviously PV gets bigger when E grows faster—companies that grow earnings faster are worth more.

The constant growth equation is a derivative of the Discounted Cash Flow Model that determines the net present value of a perpetual cash flow assuming a constant rate of growth. Instead of assuming different levels of earnings in each period, it assumes a constant growth rate off the base year and a constant cost of capital. If you are so inclined, you can wade through the derivation of the constant growth formula in the next two equations, but it is really not necessary. The discounted cash flow model, where E is cash flow and C is cost of capital:

$$PV = \sum E_1/(1 + C)^1 + E_2/(1 + C)^2 + \cdots + E_n/(1 + C)^n$$

If you assume that E grows at a constant rate (G),

$$PV = \sum (E_0 \times (1 + G)^1)/(1 + C)^1 + (E_0 \times (1 + G)^2)/(1 + C)^2$$
$$+ \cdots + (E_0 \times (1 + G)^n)/(1 + C)^n$$

the result then simplifies to:

$$PV = E/(C - G)$$

Note that if G is zero then we are back to the perpetuity formula, PV = E/C. This equation is not a theory; it is a proven mathematical concept found in most corporate finance textbooks.

We can easily apply this equation to valuing companies or valuing the entire Standard & Poor's (S&P) 500 Index by substituting operating earnings for E as a proxy for cash flow. I apply it to market valuation by substituting S&P operating earnings for cash flow and since we are talking about the price of an index, for clarity, we will use P instead of PV. The formula becomes:

$$P = E/(C - G)$$

where:

P = Price (value of S&P 500 Index).
E = Earnings (reported operating earnings for the prior four quarters as reported by S&P) as a proxy for cash flow.
G = Expected long-term growth rate.
C = Cost of capital (we will derive C in a later chapter).

This formula can also be restated to predict P/E ratio as:

$$P/E = 1/(C - G)$$

These are the two most important equations in this book. Together, these equations are useful in understanding valuation for an individual company or the market overall and, as will be discussed, with the right assumptions offer a powerful explanation for overall market levels.

NOT THE FIRST TO TRY THIS

I am not the first to try applying a constant growth equation to the stock market, but I may be the first to have done it successfully. The key is in the underlying assumptions used as inputs for E, C, and G. Some suggest that cash flow should be used and earnings are the wrong measure. While cash flow would technically be better, it is useful in a perpetuity formula only after normalizing so that it represents ongoing future cash flow. Because annual operating cash flow includes capital expenditures and other investments along with changes in working capital, cash taxes, and other balance sheet items, it is almost never a good representation of expected long-term future cash flow in a single year. While we could adjust cash flow to account for these, and we should when looking at a single company, it is impractical to do so for an entire index like the S&P 500.

I argue that when looking at the S&P 500 as a whole, these things net out. Depreciation for the S&P 500 is a good proxy for capital expenditures, so that operating earnings, which exclude nonrecurring items, is good proxy for cash flow. In short, operating earnings for the S&P 500 contain enough adjustments to be a good proxy for long-term cash flow, and that makes it a good basis for evaluating current market value. It also has the advantage of being reported frequently and has a history going back at least 50 years.

Others suggest equity should be valued as the present value of dividend payments, not earnings or cash flow. They use a version of the constant growth model called the Gordon Growth Model or Dividend Growth Model by using dividends in place of earnings. They argue that the value of equity should relate to actual cash flow received by shareholders. Some advocate a modified approach that uses dividends, plus share repurchases. One well-known advocate of this approach is Nobel Laureate Paul Krugman, who said:

> Now earnings are not the same as dividends, by a long shot; and what a stock is worth is the present discounted value of the dividends on that stock—period, end of story.[1]

Krugman is adamant that the only things that you should count are dividends and share repurchases. I disagree, and so do some of his fellow Nobel Prize winners. First, as posited by Franco Modigliani and Merton Miller in their famous article on the "irrelevance" of dividend policy, it is the underlying expected earnings power of companies, not their dividend payouts that determine corporate market values. Dividend policy does not impact valuation.[2] Dividend policy is a matter of capital structure in that companies use dividends to repatriate cash to shareholders or choose not to pay dividends in order to reinvest in their business.

Shareholders can mimic the result of dividend or share repurchases by choosing to sell shares and therefore determine the time at which they receive cash. In other words, if they want their earnings distributed in cash, they can sell shares. Why would it matter who is repurchasing the shares? Consider the examples in Table 1.2 of a company that has earnings per share (EPS) of $2, growing at 8 percent per year. We assume it trades at a P/E ratio of 20 throughout the period, so starting with earnings of $2 per share and a P/E of 20, it trades for $40 per share. Two investors each hold 1,000 shares. Investor 1 holds all his shares throughout the period.

Investor 2 makes his own dividend policy by selling shares equal to earnings—effectively mimicking a 100 percent dividend payout ratio. In the first year, he held 1,000 shares. Since the company earned $2 per share, he needed to sell $2,000 worth of shares ($2 × 1,000 shares) to create his "dividend," so he sells 50 shares ($40/share × 50 shares) to reduce his holdings to 950 shares worth $38,000.

Since we are assuming that earnings grow at 8 percent and the P/E is a constant, the share price also grows at 8 percent. If we assume that Investor 2 reinvests his distribution, also at an 8 percent return, the line FV of

TABLE 1.2 Equivalence of Selling Shares Instead of Dividends

	Year 1	Year 2	Year 3	Year 4	Year 5
EPS	2.00	2.16	2.33	2.52	2.72
P/E	20	20	20	20	20
Share Price	$40.00	$43.20	$46.66	$50.39	$54.42
Investor 1—No Distributions					
Shares	1,000	1,000	1,000	1,000	1,000
Value	$40,000	$43,200	$46,656	$50,388	$54,420
Investor 2—Distribute Earnings					
Beginning Shares	1,000	950	903	857	815
EPS on Shares Owned/Distribution	2,000	2,052	2,105	2,160	2,216
Shares to Sell	50	48	45	43	41
Ending Shares	950	903	857	815	774
Ending Value	$38,000	$38,988	$40,002	$41,042	$42,109
FV of Distributions @ 8%	$2,721	$2,585	$2,456	$2,333	$2,216
Total Distributions					$12,311
Shares + FV Distributions					$54,420

Distributions in Table 1.2 shows their value in year 5. It's not a coincidence that the ending value of shares for Investor 1 and shares plus the future value of distributions in the final year for Investor 2 are both $54,420. Since the distributions earn the same rate of return as shares, they have to be equal. Differences arise only if either shares or reinvested distributions outperform one another. Earnings are as good as a distribution!

If earnings growth is greater than the reinvestment rate, then Investor 1's results would outperform Investor 2's results. For example, if the company grew earnings at a 20 percent rate during the period, then stock price would increase at 20 percent per year, so investors would be better off maintaining their investment in the company rather than selling shares. Likewise, if the company paid a dividend, then those shareholders who reinvested the dividend in the company would outperform those who took the cash. You see, it does not matter whether the company pays out cash through dividends or share repurchases—the results are the same; since public markets provide liquidity, shareholders determine whether they will reinvest profits or not.

Furthermore, earnings are a better approximation for cash flow than dividends, which are often maintained long after earnings have declined or not paid at all by high-growth companies. Finally, information on current business condition is much stronger in earnings than in dividends, even including potential signaling with a cut or increase in dividends, and thus provide a much better gauge of future growth prospects. These contribute to making earnings a good measure.

$P = E/(C - G)$ is the key to understanding the stock market. If you understand this formula, you can understand changes in the market. We've discussed E, and in subsequent chapters we will learn how to calculate C and determine estimates for G.

WHY GROWTH RATE AND COST OF CAPITAL MATTER

The constant growth equation is helpful in understanding what drives value. Assume you have an asset (which could be a business or the entire market) with a cost of capital of 12 percent, a growth rate of 2 percent and cash flow of $100, then: P = $100/(12 percent – 2 percent) = $1,000.

The equation tells us with constant 2 percent growth in cash flow your asset is worth $1,000. This is called *intrinsic value*. We can also apply this to a share of stock to determine its intrinsic value. Instead of cash flow, we use EPS of $2 and the same cost of capital and growth rate, so the result P is now share price: P = $2/(12 percent – 2 percent) = $20. Since EPS is $2 and price is $20, the P/E is $20/$2, or a P/E of 10. While the market may value it differently, if these assumptions are true, this formula tell us its intrinsic value—its actual worth.

P/E is often used to gauge whether share price is expensive or cheap; a P/E of 8 is considered very low, but when Google had a P/E of 60 or more, some thought it was very high. Is a company with a P/E of 10 a bargain compared to a company with a P/E of 20? We can explore this question using the constant growth equation. Take the same company and now assume that its cost of capital drops from 10 percent to 8 percent and its growth rate increases from 2 percent to 3 percent and earnings stay the same. These might seem like small differences, but the impact is dramatic. P = $2/(8 percent – 3 percent) = $40, with the P/E rising to 20. The same company with a lower cost of capital and better growth doubles in value. If growth increased to 5 percent (in line with nominal long-term gross domestic product (GDP) growth) the share price rises to $66, a P/E of 33. Table 1.3 provides additional examples of how P/E varies based on growth for a company with an 8 percent cost of capital:

The formula $P = E/(C - G)$ shows that earnings relate directly to price. What many managers fail to realize is that investors don't look at earnings

TABLE 1.3 Growth Drives P/E

Growth	P/E
0%	12.6
2%	16.7
4%	25
6%	50

Note: Assumes 8% cost of capital.

in a vacuum; they parse the information in earnings in order to estimate growth. So the reporting of earnings often causes the P/E to change.

P/E RATIO EXPANSION AND CONTRACTION

P/E ratios for a company and the entire market change over time. One important use for the constant growth equation is in illustrating the probable causes of these changes:

P/E expansion. If the P/E ratio increases, it means that either earnings are expected to grow at a faster rate or cost of capital has decreased.

P/E contraction. If the P/E ratio decreases it means that either earnings are expected to grow more slowly or the cost of capital has increased.

These can be illustrated with a few simple examples. If a company has a stock price of $40 and consensus or expected earnings of $4, then it trades at a forward P/E of 10. If the company positively surprises the market by reporting earnings of $4.40, and the P/E stayed at 10, then stock price would increase to $44 (10 × $4.40). Since this was also a positive surprise, the market may also increase its growth expectations for the company which causes the P/E multiple to increase as well. If the P/E increases to 11, then the stock price increases to $48 ($4.40 × 11). Later in the book, we will revisit the topic and calculate expected growth.

If the company surprises on the other end with lower-than-expected earnings, then the opposite result ensues. Suppose they report $3.60, 10 percent below expected; then, if the P/E stays at 10, price drops to $36, but may drop more if P/E shrinks because of reduced growth expectations. Growth expectations are the reason that a stock may drop significantly when the company misses earnings by just a penny or two.

You have probably noticed that I am cautious in my language by saying "may increase" or "may decrease." This is because earnings are just part of the story. Investors will try to understand the entire story by, among other things, looking at the quality and sustainability of earnings, revenues, margins, product mix and investment. If a company reports earnings growth, they want to understand if those earnings really are representative of the future and if the company can keep growing. This will be discussed in more detail later.

CAPM, RISK PREMIUM, AND VALUATION

The Capital Asset Pricing Model (CAPM) can be used to determine the cost of equity for an individual firm or the market overall.

$$\text{Cost of Equity} = R_f + \beta \times (\text{ERP})$$

where

R_f = Risk-free rate (10-year or 30-year Treasury yields are used as a proxy).

β = Beta, the sensitivity to market risk (by definition for the entire market, it is 1.0).

ERP = Equity risk premium (this will be the main subject and the most innovative part of this discussion).

Simplifying this equation, cost of equity for the market as a whole, $C = R_f + \text{ERP}$.

The model was introduced by Jack Treynor (1961, 1962), William Sharpe (1964), John Lintner (1965), and Jan Mossin (1966) independently, building on the earlier work of Harry Markowitz. Sharpe received the Nobel Memorial Prize in Economics in 1990 (jointly with Markowitz and Merton Miller) for this contribution to the field of financial economics. While the risk-free rate is easily determined, the risk premium is not. In fact, there is no consensus. The next section will discuss some classic approaches. Later, I will discuss my suggested approach.

EQUITY RISK PREMIUM

The ERP is the expected return an investor requires above the risk-free rate for investing in a portfolio of equities. It makes sense that if 10-year Treasury yields represent the safest long-term investment (risk free), then in order to invest in something with more risk, like corporate bonds or equities, investors require a premium. My experience valuing businesses showed me how important this number can be; valuations change dramatically based on ERP assumptions. This is discussed further in the next section (Impact of Risk Premium on Market Valuation). Overall, the equity risk premium is also an important number in corporate finance, corporate decision making, regulatory matters such as utility rates, and investment analysis. Because of its importance and in order to reign in the divergent methodologies, some jurisdictions explicitly specify the method. For example, Utah specifies the exact method for determining the risk premium for property apprasials:

> *The risk premium shall be the arithmetic average of the spread*
> *between the return on stocks and the income return on long term*
> *bonds for the entire historical period contained in the Ibbotson*
> *Yearbook published immediately following the lien date.*[3]

The most common approach for determining ERP is to measure the historical premiums that investors have received relative to Treasury yields and assume that investors will expect that rate of return in the future. This method is very sensitive to the dates selected for measuring the growth, since different periods show different returns. Because the goal is to measure expectations, some argue that recent periods are more relevant, while others argue that using long-term return going back to the 1920s is the best measure.

There is also disagreement on whether to use geometric or arithmetic means for calculation. The geometric method uses the difference in compound growth rates, while the arithmetic takes the annual returns in each year, then averages them. Depending on method and time period, this can range from 3 percent to more than 7 percent. Other methods include surveys and forward-looking estimates based on current stock market levels. There is a huge body of research on measuring risk premiums. Books have been written on the equity risk premium. For example, UCLA professor Bradford Cornell wrote *The Equity Risk Premium: The Long-Run Future of the Stock Market* in 1999.[4] *Cost of Capital* by Shannon P. Pratt and Roger Grabowski devotes considerable space just to the equity risk premium.[5]

In the survey approach, a range of corporate executives, investors, and academics are asked what risk premium they are currently using. For example, Pablo Fernandez, Professor of Corporate Finance, IESE Business School, published, "Market Risk Premium Used in 2010 by Analysts and Companies: A Survey with 2,400 Answers" in May 2010.[6] They found the average in the United States was 5.1 percent for analysts and 5.3 percent for corporate participants. The spread was even larger in Europe and the United Kingdom, with 5.0 percent in Europe and 5.2 percent in the United Kingdom for analysts and 5.7 percent and 5.6 percent for corporate practitioners in Europe and the United Kingdom, respectively. The large spread between equity analysts and corporate is interesting, since it would tend to bias equity analysts toward higher valuations than their corporate counterparts. Despite the intuitive appeal of surveys, they are not used frequently.

The implied approach typically uses a variation of the constant growth equation ($P = E/(C - G)$). Using a current index price, it solves for C, using the current level of earnings, dividends or cash flow and current price. The current risk-free rate is subtracted from C to arrive at the risk premium. The approach is very sensitive to estimates of G and sometimes relies on analysts estimate. Since it is entirely dependent on current price of the index (P), it implies high risk premium when the P is high, and low when P is low. It tells us nothing about current price relative to fair value or the drivers of the risk premium.

The effort devoted to evaluating different methods and the large variation in estimates suggests that despite the importance of the ERP, current methods are not satisfactory.

IMPACT OF RISK PREMIUM ON VALUATION

Despite the considerable effort devoted to calculating the ERP, most currently accepted methods produce a huge variation in result. This has a huge impact on valuation—decreasing ERP from 7 percent to 3 percent more than doubles value. (I suspect this contributes to some distrust of DCF valuations.) Table 1.4 demonstrates the impact different ERP assumptions (3 percent – 7 percent) can have on valuation as illustrated by the P/E. Using the constant growth model, where $P/E = 1/(C - G)$, if we assume that the market will grow with long-term estimates of real GDP at 2.6 percent plus long-term inflation at 2 percent, our estimate of stock market P/E would

TABLE 1.4 ERP Drives Valuation

R_f	ERP	Cost of Equity	GDP + Inflation	Predicted P/E
5.0%	3.0%	8.0%	4.6%	29.4
5.0%	4.0%	9.0%	4.6%	22.7
5.0%	5.0%	10.0%	4.6%	18.5
5.0%	6.0%	11.0%	4.6%	15.6
5.0%	7.0%	12.0%	4.6%	13.5

have P/E $= 1/(C - 4.6$ percent). (*Note:* Real GDP + Inflation is nominal GDP). If Treasury yields are currently 5 percent, then our range of cost of capital (R_f + ERP) is 8 percent – 12 percent. Table 1.4 shows the P/E implied for the overall market in this range.

To put this in perspective, if the S&P 500 were at 800 with a P/E of 13.5, it would more than double to 1,741 with a P/E of 29.4 and the same level of earnings!

Many researchers have argued that the equity risk premium changes over time—and that such fluctuations are a major source of stock price changes—and also that the ERP has experienced a "secular" decline during the past few decades. In *Dow 36,000*, Kevin Hassett (no relation) and James Glassman argued that the risk premium was declining because investors were viewing stocks as less risky. They went so far as to suggest that that the risk premium could vanish entirely since, given a sufficient amount of time, stocks appeared virtually certain to outperform bonds.[7] In *The Myth of the Rational Market,* Justin Fox quotes Eugene Fama, one of the pioneers of the efficient market hypothesis as saying, "My own view is that the risk premium has gone down over time basically because we've convinced people that it's there."[8] Ibbotson suggested that the decline in the risk premium is a onetime event. "We think of it as a windfall that you shouldn't get again," he said.[9] I think Glassman and Hassett were right about the decline in the ERP, but not about the underlying cause.

CHAPTER RECAP

The constant growth formula is the key to understanding stock market value. With S&P operating earnings used as a proxy for cash flow, the constant growth equation can be used to estimate market value or P/E ratios by capitalizing current earnings as a perpetuity.

Two forms of the equation are:

$$P = E/(C - G)$$
$$P/E = 1/(C - G)$$

where

P = Price (value of S&P 500 Index).
E = Earnings (reported operating earnings for the prior four quarters as reported by S&P) as a proxy for cash flow.
G = Expected long-term growth rate.
C = Cost of capital.

If you understand these two equations, you can understand the stock market. Applying the constant growth equation helps understand the impact of its inputs on value:

- Impact of changes in cost of capital and growth on value where small changes in growth or cost of capital make a big difference in value.
- Cost of capital is important, so we better get it right.
- Earnings drive value (stock price) but also contain information. While we can determine current earnings, we need to forecast growth and determine the right cost of capital.
- Changes in earnings expectations drive stock price. Exceeding expectations may increase growth expectations, resulting in a higher P/E, while missing earnings expectations could signal lower growth and result in a lower P/E.
- Cost of equity according to CAPM: Cost of Equity $= R_f + \beta \times (\text{ERP})$

where

$R_f =$ Risk-free rate (10-year or 30-year Treasury yields are used as a proxy).

$\beta =$ Beta, the sensitivity to market risk (by definition for the entire market, it is 1.0).

ERP = Equity risk premium.

- ERP estimates cover a wide range, typically 3 to 7 percent with little consensus. ERP has a huge impact on valuation. With an R_f of 5 percent, an ERP dropping from 7 percent to 3 percent would more than double stock price by increasing P/E ratios.

Exploring the Risk Premium Factor Valuation Model

CHAPTER 2

The Risk Premium Factor
Valuation Model

The Risk Premium Factor (RPF) Model proposes that the equity risk premium (ERP) is a simple function of the risk-free rate. When combined with simplifying assumptions as inputs to the constant growth equation, it explains the observed variation in ERP and changes in price-to-earnings (P/E) ratios and valuations for the Standard & Poor's (S&P) 500 over the past 50 years.

Conventional theory would hold that if the equity risk premium (ERP) were 6.0 percent and 10-year Treasury yield were 4.0 percent, then investors would expect equities to yield 10 percent, but if the 10-year Treasury were 10 percent, then investors would require a 16 percent return—a proportionately smaller premium. I argue that the ERP is not fixed as in the conventional Capital Asset Pricing Model (CAPM) and cannot be determined by looking back or projecting forward, but varies directly with the level of the risk-free rate in accordance with a risk premium factor (RPF). While this proportional RPF is fairly stable, it can and does change over longer periods of time.

To illustrate the concept, with an RPF of 1.48, equities are expected to yield 9.9 percent when Treasury yields are at 4.0 percent and 24.8 percent $(10 + 1.48 \times 10 = 24.8)$ when they are at 10 percent to provide investors with the same proportional compensation for risk. In this example, the increase in interest rates (and inflation) caused the risk premium to jump from about 6 percent to 15 percent. Notice that with this approach, the cost of capital is lower than with a fixed premium when interest rates are low, but higher than the fixed premium approach when interest rates are high. This implies that interest rates have a greater impact on valuation and market price than generally recognized.

In order to test this approach, we not only need to determine the RPF, but also determine estimates for other variables. For our long-term growth rate, we simply assume that earnings will grow at the same pace as the economy. This is broken into its components of real growth plus expected inflation. A long-term real growth forecast is provided in the annual federal budget and tends to be stable, even when the economy is not. Inflation is determined by subtracting the underlying real interest rate (the rate without inflation) from the risk-free rate. We apply this to the constant growth equation:

$$P/E = 1/(C - G) \text{ or } P = E/(C - G)$$

Variables and assumptions used are as follows:

P = Price (value of S&P 500).

E = Actual earnings (annualize operating earnings for the prior four quarters as reported by S&P). Earnings, while not ideal, are used as a proxy for cash flow and seem to work very well.

G = Expected long-term projected growth rate, which is broken down into its components of real growth and inflation, so $G = G_R + I_{LT}$.

G_R = Expected long-term real growth rate. Long-term expected real growth rate (G_R) is based on long-term gross domestic product (GDP) growth expectations on the basis that real earnings for a broad index of large-cap equities will grow with GDP over the long term. A rate of 2.6 percent is used, with the same rate applied historically.[1]

Int_R = Expected real interest rate (Int_R) is 2%; based on the average 10-year Treasury Inflation-Protected Securities (TIPS) Yields from March 2003 to the present[2].

I_{LT} = Expected long-term inflation, as determined by subtracting long-term expected real interest rates (Int_R) from the 10-year Treasury.

C = Cost of capital is derived using the CAPM, where for the broad market, $C = R_f + ERP$.

R_f = Risk-free rate as measured using 10-year Treasury yields.

ERP = Risk premium factor (RPF) × R_f.

RPF = 1.24 for 1960 to 1980; 0.90 for 1981 to 2001; and 1.48 for 2002 to the present. The RPF for each period was arrived at using a linear regression to fit the assumptions above to actual P/E.

Including all assumptions, the formula reduces as follows:

$$P = E/(C - G)$$
$$P = E/(R_f + ERP - (I_{LT} + G_R))$$

$$P = E/(R_f + R_f \times RPF) - (I_{LT} + G_R)$$

$$P = E/(R_f \times (1 + RPF) - ((R_f - 2.0\,\text{percent}) + 2.6\,\text{percent}))$$

Further simplification and applying the current RPF:

$$P = E/(R_f \times (1 + 1.48) - R_f + 2.0\,\text{percent} - 2.6\,\text{percent})$$

or

$$P/E = 1/(R_f \times (1 + 1.48) - R_f + 2.0\% - 2.6\%)$$

Note that you can reduce the constant to 0.6 percent results from subtracting the assumed long-term real interest rate of 2 percent from the long-term growth rate of 2.6 percent.

Don't sweat it if you don't follow the math. The important takeaway is in the last two lines, where the only variables left are the risk-free rate (R_f), which is the current yield on long-term Treasuries; the RPF, which is 1.48; and S&P operating earnings. For the most part, the model says that the P/E for the S&P 500 is determined entirely by the risk-free rate and the index value is P/E times S&P operating earnings. Everything necessary to determine fair value is readily available and easily calculated.

THE RPF MODEL IS SIMPLE, BUT DOES IT WORK?

In order to demonstrate the effectiveness of the model, I've charted the predicted versus actual P/E and index level for the S&P 500. The data goes back 50 years to 1960 on an annual basis and 1986 on a monthly and quarterly basis. In each of the charts below, the actual deviated significantly from the predicted at year-end 2008 and for the quarter ending March 31, 2009, but came back into parity by June 2009. I believe this was due to the abnormally low yields for long Treasuries that had been in effect since late 2008, where the "flight to quality" as a safe haven, combined with the Federal Reserve's purchase of notes beginning in March 2009, caused Treasuries to be overpriced.[3] Yields on the 10-year had been 2.2 to 2.7 percent, compared to a range of 4.1 to 5.1 percent in 2006 and 2007 and rarely less than 4 percent since 1960. Yields for the 10-year during this period are shown in Figure 2.1.

To compensate for these abnormally low Treasury yields, I have indicated the P/E result if Treasury yields were at a still low, but more normal, yield of 4 percent. This normalization of the R_f causes the predicted value to correspond closely with actual valuations. In the monthly and quarterly charts, I substituted the 30-year Treasury yield for the 10-year beginning

FIGURE 2.1   10-Year Treasury Yields, 1962 to 2011
Source: U.S. Treasury, H.15 Selected Interest Rates. Accessed March 2010 to February 2011, at www.federalreserve.gov/datadownload/Choose.aspx?rel=H.15.

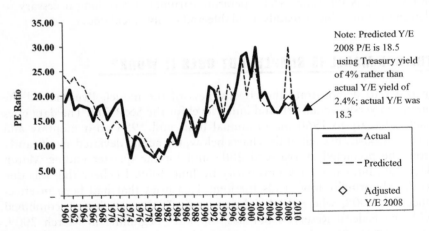

FIGURE 2.2   S&P 500 P/E Actual vs. Predicted 1960 to 2010 (Annual)
Source: S&P earnings and price from 1988 to present from Standard & Poor's web site (www.standardandpoors.com/indices/sp-500/en/us/?indexId=spusa-500-usduf–p-us-l–); S&P averages 1960 to 1987 from Damodaran Online: Home page for Answath Damodaran, New York University (http://pages.stern.nyu.edu/ ~adamodar/); Treasury yields from Federal Reserve, H.15 Selected Interest Rates (www.federalreserve.gov/datadownload/Choose.aspx?rel=H.15).

in 2008 when the spread between 10-year and 30-year became historically large. As of November 2009, it was 130 basis points (bps) or 44 percent greater—its largest ever. This is compared to a historical average of 20 bps or just 4 percent. One use of the model is to spot anomalies; I believe this was an anomaly.

Figure 2.2 shows P/E ratio calculated using the assumptions described above for 1960 to 2010.[4] It clearly shows the decline in P/Es during the 1970s and the rise in the 1980s, demonstrating that the model has good explanatory power of the changes. Figure 2.3 show monthly data for 1986 to December 2010[5] with the actual and predicted came back into parity by the quarter ending June 2009. The RPF model explains overall market

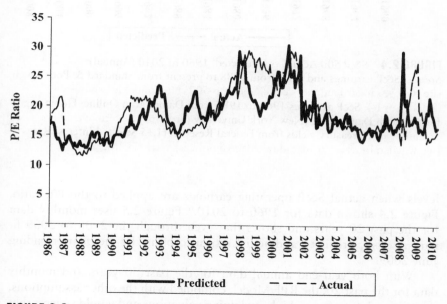

FIGURE 2.3 S&P 500 P/E Actual vs. Predicted, 1986 to February 2011 (Monthly)
Source: S&P earnings and price from 1988 to present from Standard & Poor's web
site (www.standardandpoors.com/indices/sp-500/en/us/?indexId=spusa-500-
usduf–p-us-l–); S&P monthly earnings for 1/86 to 11/88 from "Online Data Robert
Shiller" (www.econ.yale.edu/-shiller/data.htm); Treasury yields from Federal
Reserve, H.15 Selected Interest Rates (www.federalreserve.gov/
datadownload/Choose.aspx?rel=H.15). Because earnings are released quarterly, the
model was extended to monthly and daily price data by using operating earnings as
a constant for each month in the quarter applied for the month preceding
quarter-end (i.e., December to February = Q1) under the assumption that market
expectations would have incorporated earning expectations.

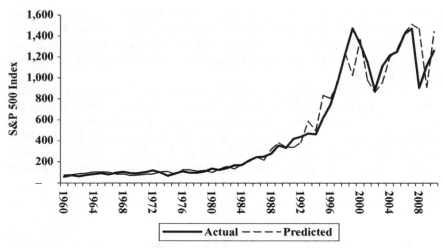

FIGURE 2.4 S&P 500 Actual vs. Predicted, 1960 to 2010 (Annual)
Source: S&P earnings and price from 1988 to present from Standard & Poor's web site (www.standardandpoors.com/indices/sp-500/en/us/?indexId=spusa-500-usduf–p-us-l–); S&P averages 1960 to 1987 from Damodaran Online: Home page for Answath Damodaran (New York University (http://pages.stern.nyu.edu/~adamodar/); Treasury yields from Federal Reserve, H.15 Selected Interest Rates (www.federalreserve.gov/datadownload/Choose.aspx?rel=H.15).

levels when actual S&P operating earnings are applied to the P/E ratio. Figure 2.4 shows data for 1960 to 2010.[6] Figure 2.5 uses monthly data for the past 20 years and shows that even through the 2008 to 2009 financial crisis, predicted and actual return to parity by the quarter ending June 2009.

With both year-end annual data for the past 50 years and monthly data for the past 20, the RPF Model, combined with the other assumptions, appears to do a very good job explaining valuations and would suggest that at any point in time, just two factors, interest rates, and earnings explain P/E ratios and index levels.

ESTIMATING THE RPF

This section discusses the methodology for estimating the actual factor. If you are not interested in the derivations, then go ahead and skip this section. As discussed, the RPF Model was devised to explain price movements and

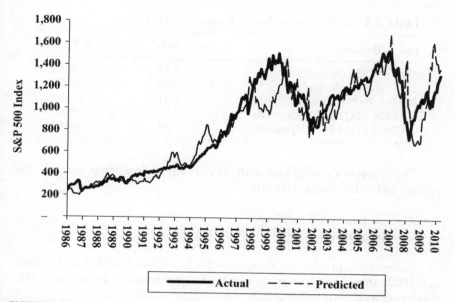

FIGURE 2.5 S&P 500 Actual vs. Predicted, 1986 to February 2011 (Monthly)
Source: S&P earnings and price from 1988 to present from Standard & Poor's web
site (www.standardandpoors.com/indices/sp-500/en/us/?indexId=spusa-500-
usduf–p-us-l–); S&P monthly earnings for 1/86 to 11/88 from "Online Data Robert
Shiller" (www.econ.yale.edu/-shiller/data.htm); Treasury yields from Federal
Reserve, H.15 Selected Interest Rates (www.federalreserve.gov/
datadownload/Choose.aspx?rel=H.15). Because earnings are released quarterly, the
model was extended to monthly and daily price data by using operating earnings as
a constant for each month in the quarter applied for the month preceding quarter
end (i.e., December to February = Q1) under the assumption that market
expectations would have incorporated earning expectations.

current value of the S&P 500. While the overall construct of the model is
based on valuation theory, thus not a black box model, the actual RPF was
derived using linear regression in order to find the best fit over long periods.
In order to perform the regression, I applied a transformation to isolate
interest rates as the independent variable as follows:

$$P = E/(R_f \times (1 + RPF) - (R_f - Int_R) - 2.6\%)$$
$$E/P = R_f \times (1 + RPF) - (R_f - Int_R) - 2.6\%$$
$$R_f \times (1 + RPF) = E/P + (R_f - 2.0\%) - 2.6\%$$

TABLE 2.1   RPF Valuation Model R-Squared Results

Period/Dataset	RPF	R-Squared
1960 to 1980 (Annual)	1.24	98.4%
1981 to 2001 (Annual)	0.90	99.7%
2002 to 2008 (Annual)	1.51	98.8%
Q4 1986 to Q2 2002 (Quarterly)	0.90	99.6%
Q3 2002 to Q3 2008 (Quarterly)	1.48	99.8%

The regressions were run with RPF as the independent variable and applied to the following data sets:

- Annual data: 1960 to 2008
- Quarterly data: Q4 1986 to Q4 2008

As described in other sections, since the RPF shifted in 1981 and September 2002, these data sets were ultimately segmented at those dates. The results are as shown in Table 2.1.

These factors were then applied to the final model (as opposed to the transformed equation) and full data set in order to select the best factor.[7] The RPF was estimated by fitting the model to actual S&P levels. This analysis revealed two distinct shifts in the RPF since 1960. Table 2.2 shows the RPF factors that provided the best fit for each period.

The overall fit was assessed by calculating the R-squared using the appropriate RPF for each time period. As previously discussed, the meltdown post–September 2008 drove down the risk-free rate to an unsustainable level and left a trail of historical earnings that clearly did not reflect expectations. As also discussed previously, these factors are now back in line. To adjust for this recent anomaly, the R-squared was calculated excluding the meltdown time period beginning September 2008. The results are shown in Table 2.3.

Excluding the meltdown period, where one should reasonably substitute expected earnings and risk-free rate, the RPF Valuation Model explains

TABLE 2.2   Estimated Risk Premium Factors

Period	RPF
1960 to 1980	1.24
1981 to Q2 2002	0.90
Q3 2002 to Present	1.48

TABLE 2.3　RPF Valuation Model R-Squared Results

	R-Squared	
Dataset	Full Dataset	Excluding Meltdown
1960 to 2008 (Annual)	89.5%	96.3%
1986 to September 2009 (Quarterly)	80.6%	88.0%
January 1986 to September 2009 (Monthly)	86.2%	90.8%
January 1986 to September 2009 (Daily)	86.5%	90.9%

96 percent variation of stock prices over the past 50 years and 91 percent of the daily variation.[8]

POTENTIAL CAUSES FOR SHIFTS IN THE RPF

The RPF has shifted twice in the past 50 years, once in 1981 and again in July 2002. The period from 1960 to 1981 was characterized by increasing inflation expectations rising from 1.8 percent in 1960 to 11.7 percent in 1981.[9] In 1981 the trend reversed and inflation expectations began to decline. The 1981 shift in RPF from 1.24 to 0.9 could have resulted from this change in inflation expectations driven by world events with the decline in inflation resulting in higher real after-tax equity returns. Events during 1981 that could have contributed this change include:

- *January 19:* Iran hostage crisis ends. The reduction of tensions could have increased expectations of stability and a secure oil supply bringing with it lower inflation and less risk of an economic shock.[10]
- *January 20:* Reagan inaugurated and begins to reduce taxes, resulting in higher real after-tax returns.

The RPF increased from 0.9 to 1.48 in mid-2002. The declining rate of long-term inflation ceased in 2002, with long-term inflation expectations having declined from a peak of 11.7 percent in 1981 to 2.0 percent in 2002. The rate remained stable from 2002 to 2008, fluctuating in the 2 to 3 percent range. Other events that could have caused or contributed to the shift in 2002 were:

- *January:* Department of Justice announces investigation into Enron. Enron, Tyco, and WorldCom's destruction of confidence in reported earnings could have led to increased RPF.[11]

- *July:* Sarbanes-Oxley enacted in response to accounting scandals. The act faced severe criticism for imposing significant costs on public companies. Some suggested high compliance costs would cause capital to flee to less regulated markets, increasing the premium required for U.S. equities.[12]
- *October:* Congress authorizes war in Iraq (opposite of 2002). Expectation that we will enter protracted war with Iraq could have heightened expectations that increased borrowing to fund the war would lead to increased inflation and tax rates in the future.[13]

POTENTIAL WEAKNESSES IN RPF THEORY AND METHODOLOGY

Proper application of the model requires an understanding of its potential weaknesses:

- **All data points are current actual or historical.** The market is forward looking, yet all data in the analysis is based on actual historical data. Even 10-year Treasury yields, which inherently embody future expectations for real interest and inflation, were sampled at a single point in time, along with earnings, which are not released until well after the quarter ends. Analysts' estimates are widely accepted as being embodied in current share price and would be expected to be reasonably close to actual before the end of each quarter.
- **Reasons for changes in RPF are not fully explained.** The RPF has changed twice over the past 50 years and has historically held for long periods of time. While I have offered a number of suggested reasons for the two changes in the RPF over the past 50 years, it is clear that further explanation and understanding would be beneficial.
- **The RPF may seem to be set arbitrarily to fit actual.** While not completely alleviating this concern with the good linear regression fit across a relatively large number of data points, the RPF seems to make sense and provide good results.
- **RPF cannot be projected.** In order for this to be most useful for investors, we need to have confidence in the RPF. Thus far, it seems possible to discern the RPF only in hindsight. Still, this would seem superior to other methods for determining risk premiums that produce less definitive results. For example, if the RPF changed just two times over 50 years, one might argue that in any year there is a 96 percent chance (48 out of 50) that the RPF will remain constant over the next year.

ADJUSTED RISK-FREE RATE

The model was originally constructed using the 30-year Treasury as the risk free rate back in 1999 because I believe the 30-year better reflects long-term inflation expectations and risk embodied in equities. From March 2002 through the end of 2005, the 30-year rate was not reported, so I converted my analysis to use the 10-year, which has data going back to the early 1950s. During 2008 to 2011, due to Fed buying (quantitative easing) and some flight to quality, rates on the 10-year became especially depressed. This is evidenced by the spread between the 10-year and 30-year reaching more than 130 bps or 44 percent greater—its largest spread ever. Historically, the average spread was just 20 bps or 4 percent. Since the 30-year yield is also probably depressed by the Fed buying, I have substituted the 30-year yield in most examples for the risk-free rate for 2008 to 2011. This includes most examples in this book, other than the preceding R-squared analysis. (You could make a case for using 96 percent of the 30-year if you believed that the 30-year was fairly priced.)

As shown in Table 2.4, the 30-year actually improves the fit of the model when applied during this period.

TABLE 2.4 RPF Valuation Model R-Squared Results with 30-year as R_f for 2008 to 2011

	R-Squared	
Dataset	Full Dataset	Excluding Meltdown
1960 to 2008 (Annual)	93.8%	96.7%
1986 to September 2009 (Quarterly)	86.1%	89.2%
January 1986 to September 2009 (Monthly)	90.0%	91.9%
January 1986 to September 2009 (Daily)	89.7%	90.9%

COMPARISON TO THE FED MODEL

The RPF Model is not based on the Fed Model. It is similar, but I had not heard of the Fed Model until a few years after I began working on the RPF Model and did not begin to explore it in depth until I began writing this book. While the Fed Model was not an influence on my development of the RPF Model, some discussion is warranted since the models share a common premise—investors expect a return proportionate to the risk-free rate.

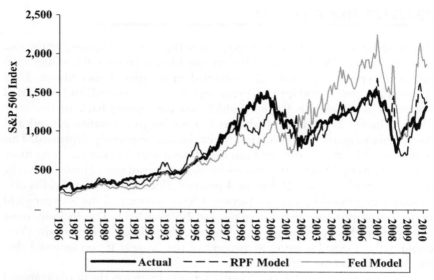

FIGURE 2.6 RPF vs. Fed Model
Source: S&P earnings and price from 1988 to present from Standard & Poor's
web site (www.standardandpoors.com/indices/sp-500/en/us/?indexId=spusa-500-
usduf–p-us-l–); S&P monthly earnings for 1/86 to 11/88 from "Online Data
Robert Shiller" (www.econ.yale.edu/-shiller/data.htm_; Treasury Yields from
Federal Reserve, H.15 Selected Interest Rates (www.federalreserve.gov/
datadownload/Choose.aspx?rel=H.15). Because earnings are released quarterly,
the model was extended to monthly and daily price data by using operating
earnings as a constant for each month in the quarter applied for the month
preceding quarter end (i.e., December to February = Q1) under the assumption
that market expectations would have incorporated earning expectations.

The Fed Model is thought to have gained its name from a July 1997
Federal Reserve Monetary Policy Report that was referenced by Prudential
Securities strategist Ed Yardeni in 1997.[14] While not an official Fed model,
the name stuck and has generated significant discussion and analysis. The
report suggested that stock prices might be overvalued since "the yield on
ten-year Treasury notes now exceeds the ratio of 12-month-ahead earnings
to prices by the largest amount since 1991."[15] The model suggests that
dividends or earnings yield (the inverse of P/E) should equal the nominal
yield on 10-year Treasuries. Alternatively, the market P/E should equal the
inverse of the 10-year Treasury yield. Predicted value for the S&P 500 based
on the Fed Model would be:

$$P = E/R_f$$

Figure 2.6 compares the predicted values from the RPF Model and the Fed Model from 1986 through early 2011. While the Fed model does show correlation with the market, results are clearly not as good as the RPF Model.

Much of the discussion has suggested that the Fed Model works only because investors incorrectly account for inflation by applying a nominal discount rate to cash flows that do not reflect the same level of inflation implied by the risk-free rate.[16] Others have concluded that although there is some relationship between earnings and interest rates, there is no cause-and-effect relationship, and to imply one fails on theoretical grounds. For example, in his critique of the Fed Model, Clifford Asness suggests that inflation should not impact value because any earnings growth would be offset by a higher discount rate.[17] These analyses miss the key insight of the RPF Model—that the risk premium is proportionate to the risk-free rate, so that values rise and fall with inflation. The RPF Model shows why the relationships suggested by the Fed Model actually work in theory as well as practice.

CHAPTER RECAP

The equity risk premium varies with the risk-free rate times a factor called the risk premium factor (RPF). The RPF Model is a combination of the constant growth equation, the RPF, and some simplifying assumptions. When combined with the simplifying assumptions as inputs to the constant growth equation, it explains the variation in ERP over the past 50 years, including the observed decline in ERP and overall valuations for the S&P 500.

- ERP = Risk premium factor (RPF) $\times$ R_f.
- The 10-year Treasury yield was used as R_f to estimate RPF.
- The 30-year yield has been used as R_f in the RPF Model since 2008 because of the unusually large spread between 30-year and 10-year yields.
- RPF is currently 1.48 but has shifted twice since 1960.

Period	RPF
1960 to 1980	1.24
1981 to Q2 2002	0.90
Q3 2002 to Present	1.48

- The R-squared on a monthly basis from 1986 to 2009 excluding melt-down is over 90 percent, and over 96 percent on an annual basis since 1960.
- The RPF Model reduces to:

$$P = E/(R_f \times (1 + 1.48) - (R_f - 2.0\% + 2.6\%)) \text{ or}$$

$$P/E = 1/(R_f \times (1 + 1.48) - (R_f - 2.0\% + 2.6\%))$$

One very important takeaway is that the model says that the P/E for the S&P 500 is determined entirely by the risk-free rate and the RPF. Everything necessary to determine fair value is readily available.

The RPF has shifted just twice in the past 50 years, but causes of the shifts are still not fully explained. Since shifts in the RPF may be unpredictable, investors still need to use caution when applying the model. However, since the RPF has shifted only twice in the past 50 years, this would seem to imply that these shifts may be rare, with perhaps only a 2 in 50 chance that it will shift in any year.

CHAPTER **3**

Solving the Equity Premium Puzzle

The Link to Loss Aversion

The Risk Premium Factor (RPF) Model solves the equity premium puzzle by demonstrating that varying the equity risk premium (ERP) with the risk-free rate is consistent with prospect theory and loss aversion.

The equity premium puzzle in considered one of the most significant questions in finance. The term *equity premium puzzle* was coined by Mehra and Prescott in their 1985 paper, "The Equity Premium, A Puzzle,"[1] referring to the inability to reconcile the observed ERP with financial models. In the analysis, they use short-term Treasuries as the risk-free rate to calculate the real return on equities over numerous historical periods. They conclude that, on average, short-term Treasuries have produced a real return of about 1 percent over the long term, while equities have yielded 7 percent, implying a premium of about 6 percent or seven times the risk free return. Unable to reconcile a 7× premium with financial models, they term it a *puzzle*.

Since then, numerous papers have also attempted to explain the difference, including Benartzi and Thaler's "Myopic Loss Aversion and the Equity Premium Puzzle,"[2] which attempts to explain it in relation of loss aversion as first described in a paper by Daniel Kahneman and Amos Tversky in 1979.[3] They state:

The second behavioral concept we employ is mental accounting [Kahneman and Tversky 1984; Thaler 1985]. Mental accounting refers to the implicit methods individuals use to code and evaluate financial outcomes: transactions, investments, gambles, etc. The aspect of mental accounting that plays a particularly important role in this research is the dynamic aggregation rules people follow. Because of the presence of loss aversion, these aggregation rules are not neutral.

Our mental accounting for gains and losses determines how we perceive them.

LOSS AVERSION

Loss aversion refers to the fact that people are more sensitive to decreases in wealth than increases—the pain of losing is greater than the joy of winning. Empirical estimates find that losses are weighted about twice as strongly as gains. Studies found that the pain of losing $100 is roughly twice the perceived benefit of gaining $100, so on average test subjects required equal odds of winning $200 to compensate for the potential loss of $100 (e.g., Kahneman and Tversky, 1992;[4] Kahneman, Knetsch, and Thaler, 1991;[5] Thaler, Tversky, Kahneman, and Schwartz, 1997[6]). In other words, the average subject required a gain of twice the potential loss to take a gamble that had equal chance of loss or gain.

This was in stark contrast to the belief that people, as rational beings, evaluated the expected value and would be indifferent to a chance of gaining $100 to losing $100 if the odds were 50/50; if the gain were tilted to be slightly favorable, they should take the bet. In reality, losing hurts more; people on average do not find the prospect of gaining $101 along with an equal chance of losing $99 to be an attractive wager. In their experiments, they found that subjects required about $200 to be willing to accept the 50/50 proposition of losing $100. For this work, Kahneman won the Nobel Prize in Economics in 2002 after Tversky passed away in 1996. Of course, all people do not behave this way all the time; otherwise, Las Vegas would not exist!

LOSS AVERSION
AND CORPORATE DECISION MAKING

Incorporating loss aversion into financial thinking is in many ways a significant departure from how finance is often taught and practiced. In business school, I was taught to rely on net present value (NPV) and expected value. A project with positive NPVs should be pursued, and when faced with a range of potential outcomes, the expected value can be calculated by assigning probabilities to each outcome. The mantra: pursue all NPV-positive projects.

My experience has been that the business world rarely works this way. Due to corporate as much as individual loss aversion, decision makers are often much more risk averse, viewing the consequence of failure much greater than the rewards for success. Investments that have only slightly positive NPV or expected value are usually not pursued. Even the more risk-tolerant individuals would tend to avoid risk if the organization takes a very dim view of loss.

This is why it is so important for organizations to employ incentive structures that reward sustainable growth in value and prudent risk taking. My own experience is that organizations without such incentives tend to be very risk averse. When decisions come down, the internal calculus that investing successfully results in no reward, where failure is career limiting or results in unemployment, investment and growth are sure to slow. I would argue also that this explains risk taking for traders on Wall Street, where outsized rewards are given for success compared to the more limited stigmas or punishments for failure. It's not that traders need high tolerance for risk, it's that when using OPM (other people's money), the penalty for failure is small.

ATTEMPTS TO SOLVE THE EQUITY PREMIUM PUZZLE

As previously discussed, Mehra and Prescott coined the phrase *equity premium puzzle* because they estimated that investors would require a very high coefficient of relative risk aversion (of the order of 40 or 50) to justify the observed ERP of 7 percent. Mehra and Prescott revisited the topic two decades later with their 2003 paper, "The Equity Premium in Retrospect,"[7] where they continued to try to solve the puzzle by comparing real returns and asked whether the equity premium is due to a premium for bearing nondiversifiable risk. They concluded the answer is no unless you assume that the individual has an extreme aversion to risk—many times higher than the $2\times$ return seen in the lab.

They approach the problem using a general equilibrium model and compared short-term real risk-free rates to observed equity premium. While I am not in a position to opine on the use of these models in evaluating equity premium, for several reasons I will discuss shortly, I believe that the use of short-term real rates is mistaken. I am not surprised they could not explain the rationale for investors to justify such a dramatic disparity because, in my opinion, they are not making the right comparison. Rather than using short-term real rates, they should have used long-term nominal rates.

What they did was a bit like measuring the speed of one moving vehicle from another moving vehicle. If car A is moving at 60 mph and car B is behind it at 66 mph and car C is next traveling at 61 mph, car C will see itself gaining on car A at just 1 mph (61 vs. 60). From the perspective of car C, car B is gaining on car A at a rate of 6 mph (66 vs. 60) or 6× faster than itself. This is all fine unless we care about their speed relative to a neutral observer who is not moving. Relative to the neutral observer, car B is going only 10 percent faster than car A.

Mehra and Prescott did not pick the right relative observation point. By using real returns they are measuring the difference from a moving vehicle by ignoring the speed of inflation. If we look at this from the perspective of real returns, then the relative premium looks huge. But if we look at it from the perspective of nominal returns, the neutral observer, then the premium is not unreasonable. This is consistent with both the way individuals have been shown to evaluate gains and losses and with financial theory.

The mental accounting of investors focuses on the nominal returns. It's what investors track and how money managers are compensated. So it makes sense that the proper basis for evaluating the risk premium relative to the risk-free rate is long-term nominal returns. For example, let's assume inflation is 2 percent. If an investor is considering a $1,000 investment with Treasuries at 4 percent, the yield is guaranteed to be $40 per year with a full return of principal. While the investor is exposed to interim fluctuations in value, the coupon and return of principal are guaranteed. Alternatively, the same investor considering an investment in the Standard & Poor's (S&P) 500 Index would be evaluating the expected return relative to the nominal long-term rate rather than the real short-term rate. In this case, expected equity returns of 10 percent would look good, yielding on average $100 per year rather than $40. If we calculate real returns by subtracting the 2 percent inflation, the $80 return for equities dwarfs the $20 for Treasuries, making the premium look high with the equity return at four times Treasuries.

Now let's assume that expected inflation rises to 6 percent and the risk-free rate jumps to 8 percent, so a new $1,000 bond would yield $80. If you applied the same 6 percent premium for equities, you get an expected yield of $140. Sure the real returns are the same, but doesn't the risky $140 look less attractive compared to a guaranteed $80? The relative real return is still 4×, but the relative nominal return will have fall from 2.5× to 1.75×.

Is nominal the right thing to track? Maybe not, but it is the reality. If investors compare their returns on equities to the nominal return of other investments, any attempt to explain the premium must compare the relative return as perceived by investors. Nominal, not real, returns should be used.

Long-term Treasury rates are used in determining cost of capital since they embody the market's best guess on long-term inflation. Even though this means they are not truly risk free, it is the best market estimate of expected interest rate and inflation risk; it is the right reference point. While it's true that using real equity returns accounts for the actual inflation component, it does not account for interest rate risk. In order account for expected inflation, most practitioners use long-term Treasuries as the risk-free rate. In doing so, they also incorporate a risk factor for interest rates.

Required return can be thought of as follows:

$$\text{Nominal Equity Return} = \text{Real Equity Return} + \text{Inflation}$$
$$= \text{Short-Term Risk-Free Rate} + \text{Inflation}$$
$$+ \text{Interest Rate Risk Premium}$$
$$+ \text{Equity Risk Premium}$$

If you subtract inflation from both sides to derive the real required return, you are still left with interest rate risk, which includes risk of un-expected inflation. So by using real equity returns and short-term risk free rate, you still have to account for the interest rate risk premium.

$$\text{Real Equity Return} = \text{Short-Term Risk Free Rate}$$
$$+ \text{Interest Rate Risk Premium}$$
$$+ \text{Equity Risk Premium}$$

Essentially, what Mehra and Prescott were calling the equity risk premium was really the equity risk premium plus the interest rate risk premium. Some believe that interest rates do not have a material impact on equity returns since inflation will result in earnings growth and since equities are priced as a multiple of earnings, as earnings grow stock prices increase with inflation. As I will discuss later, inflation has a huge impact on equity prices.

In "Myopic Loss Aversion and the Equity Premium Puzzle," Benzarti and Thaler posit that the high degree of loss aversion is due to "myopic loss aversion" in that investors are sensitive to interim losses as equity markets fluctuate. They suggest that since nominal returns are what is reported, when investors evaluate performance, they actually use nominal rather than real returns to measure performance. They find that a loss aversion factor of 2.25 to 2.78 is consistent with observed risk premiums if investors evaluate their portfolios about once a year and overall results are very sensitive to frequency of evaluation. In "The Effect of Myopia and Loss Aversion on Risk," Thaler, Tversky, Kahneman, and Schwartz looked at this question through lab experiments and found that subjects were more loss averse when they evaluated their returns more frequently and that they viewed guaranteed outcomes as a reference point with an evaluation period of about one year (13 months). In other words, investors evaluate their portfolios annually and expect a premium proportionate to the nominal risk-free rate.

The RPF Model works only if we assume that the equity risk premium is conditioned on the risk-free rate, meaning that it gets bigger when Treasury yields increase and smaller when they shrink. In fact, one reason that I suspect many studies compared real returns, rather than nominal returns, may be the belief that inflation does not impact valuation. One common belief is that since profits will grow with inflation, inflation does not matter when discounted back. Another look at the constant growth equation can help understand this thinking:

$$P/E = 1/(C - G)$$

where

$C = R_f + ERP.$
$G = \text{Real Growth} + \text{Expected Inflation}.$
$R_f = \text{Real Interest Rate} + \text{Expect Inflation}.$

We can restate the equation for P/E as:

$$P/E = 1/(\text{Real Interest Rate} + \text{Expect Inflation} + ERP)$$
$$- (\text{Real Growth} + \text{Expected Inflation})$$

Expected inflation is canceled out and:

$$P/E = 1/(\text{Real Interest Rate} + ERP + \text{Real Growth})$$

If we assume that ERP, real interest rate, and real growth are a constant over the long term, P/E is also a constant. And this would be true if the equity ERP were a constant. But if we assume that the ERP moves with the risk-free rate, then we get the relationship where predicted P/E corresponds to actual.

TABLE 3.1 Inflation Drives Valuation

Inflation	R_f	ERP	Cost of Equity	G	Predicted P/E
2.0%	4.0%	5.9%	9.9%	4.6%	18.8
3.0%	5.0%	7.4%	12.4%	5.6%	14.7
4.0%	6.0%	8.9%	14.9%	6.6%	12.1
5.0%	7.0%	10.4%	17.4%	7.6%	10.2
6.0%	8.0%	11.8%	19.8%	8.6%	8.9

IMPACT OF INFLATION ON VALUE

Some argue that inflation should not have an impact on equity values, since higher costs can be passed on in the form of higher prices, so on average, earnings growth should keep up with inflation. If you assume P/E ratios should be a constant, say, 19, then with earnings of $2 per share a company would trade at $38. With 5 percent inflation, earnings would grow to $2.10 and the share price to $39.90—a gain of 5 percent, which just matches inflation.

We get the same result using a constant growth model and a fixed ERP. Let's assume the ERP constant is 6 percent, the risk-free rate is 7 percent, which embodies 5 percent inflation, and real long-term growth rate of 2.6 percent. Using the formula P/E = 1/(C – G) we get, P/E = 1/(7 percent + 6 percent) – (5 percent + 2.6 percent) for a P/E of 18.5. If we lower the inflation rate to 2 percent, the risk-free rate drops to 4 percent and we calculate P/E = (4 percent + 6 percent) – (2 percent + 2.6 percent) = 18.5. As shown earlier, any change in inflation cancels itself out.

However, if we derive the ERP using the RPF Model instead of using a constant, then the ERP varies with inflation. More inflation results in a higher risk premium. Using a 2 percent real interest rate, Table 3.1 demonstrates the impact of inflation on P/E.

Because investors expect a proportionately higher return over risk free, as inflation rises they apply a greater discount to future earnings, resulting in a lower present value, resulting in a lower P/E multiple.

BACK TO LOSS AVERSION

We know that individuals have different tolerances for risk. If the RPF is 1.48, that implies the market as a whole has a loss aversion coefficient of 2.48. That is the average of all investors, not every individual. We would expect some to have lower coefficients and others higher. Gambling addicts destroy their own lives, knowing the odds are not better than even, implying a loss aversion coefficient of less than 1.0. Likewise, some people are more risk averse than average. This is one of the factors that act to set price.

The prices for individual stocks are set at the margin. For example, assume that Google closed today at $476 and traded about 2.5 million shares. But with 320 million shares outstanding, that is less than 1 percent. The price is set by the investors trading that 1 percent. The implication is that the owners of the remaining 99 percent think Google is worth more than the current $476 and some number of investors would be will to buy Google at a lower price. Mechanically, the way this works is that sellers offer to sell a number of shares at a certain price, called the *ask,* and potential buyers offer to buy at a specified price, called the *bid.* The bid for Google might be 200 shares at $476.07, and the ask 700 shares at $476.18. The difference, $0.11 in this case, is called the *bid-ask spread.* These are the current best offers to buy and sell. For high-volume stocks like Google, the bid-ask spread is small, just 0.02 percent in this case. For lower-volume equities the spread will generally be higher.

If an investor places a market order to, say, buy 500 shares, the first 200 shares will be filled at the current bid price for 200 shares at $476.17. The remaining 300 shares will be filled by the next best ask price, which will be $476.17 or higher. It is not the consensus or average estimate of value that determines the price, but the price at which investors at the margin are willing to buy or sell at any moment. So if I don't own shares of Google and I think it's worth just $400 or even $100, I am not a factor in setting the price. But if in the moment described above, I enter a bid for 200 shares at $476.18, the order is immediately filled and, for that moment, I am the price setter.

Similarly, investors with loss aversion coefficients at the extremes should not be expected to have much market impact. An investor with a loss aversion coefficient well above 2.5 will be risk averse and have a portfolio skewed toward government bonds, while an investor with a loss aversion coefficient near 1.0 will always have a portfolio that is mostly equities. Therefore, neither will have much impact on price setting. However, investors with loss aversion coefficients around 2.5 will be more likely to be shifting their portfolios between bonds and equities and have a larger impact on pricing.

OUR REPTILIAN BRAIN

Loss aversion is hardwired into us. Research is pointing to a part of the brain called the amygdala that sits at the center of the human brain and is associated with certain emotions, including fear, as the cause of loss aversion. When we think about losing something, the amygdala is activated.[8] It is part of the limbic system that includes all the structures involved with emotion, motivation, and the emotional associations with memory. It is thought to be part an old part of our brain in evolutionary terms and can be thought of as our reptilian brain[9] in that it controls many instinctive behaviors. More evolved (thinking) parts of our brain, like the prefrontal cortex, are responsible for cognition. We can think of the primitive brain as being responsible for instinctive and gut feelings, while the thinking part of our brain uses logic. These two systems can sometimes be in conflict with the thinking part of the brain trying to explain the signals generated by our primitive brain.

Hardwired loss aversion is clearly a benefit in many situations. In the primitive world, we might have faced many life-threatening situations where loss aversion greatly improved the odds of survival. Not just in fight-or-flight situations, but in basic hunting and gathering where protecting the food we had acquired would command a premium over seeking more food. It is not surprising that this survival behavior evolved. Consider an ancient hunter on the plains who has killed a bird that will help keep his family from starving. With this bird in hand, he spots two more and assesses that he has a 50-50 chance of procuring them, but only if he abandons the bird in hand in the hunt. We'll assume that this is an all-or-nothing proposition in that he is sure to lose his bird in hand if he sets it down to hunt the others and that if he chooses hunt, he'll get both or none. Given the significant downside in ending up without food, he might pass on this opportunity to double his birds. However, if he spotted a third bird, sweetening the pot, he might reasonably decide to take the risk. So, in this case, a bird in hand is worth three in the bush. We are programmed to value what we already have in hand and to avoid risk.

In addition to the experiments discussed earlier that described the loss aversion behavior, research seems to have also pinpointed the amygdala as the place where loss aversion sits in the human brain. Two subjects with damaged amygdalas but otherwise normal brains and brain function, including intelligence quotient (IQ) were studied. In a series of experiments that studied their level of loss aversion, the subjects with the damaged amygdalas had significantly lower risk premiums than their matched control groups.[10] Since it is our reptilian brain that causes loss aversion, by extension, it is also the reptilian brain that is responsible for the ERP and thus valuation of the entire stock market.

This contributes to what I have called the reptilian response of the stock market to simple stimuli—interest rates rise, the market falls; earnings increase, the market goes up.

CHAPTER RECAP

Loss aversion is hardwired into us and drives a number of decision processes that seems to include how investors set prices in the stock market. Many studies have attempted and failed to link loss aversion to the equity risk premium. By showing that the risk premium is proportional to Treasury yields, the RPF Model establishes the connection between loss aversion theory and the ERP using real-world evidence that the market actually behaves this way.

The RPF Model
and Major Market Events
from 1981 to 2009

The Risk Premium Factor (RPF) Model shows that more than half of the growth in the Standard & Poor's (S&P) 500 Index since 1981 can be attributed to the risk-free rate declining from its peak of 13.7 percent in 1981. The interplay between interest rates, earnings, and valuation is a useful tool for identifying bubbles and diagnosing their cause.

Interest rates are much more important than is generally recognized. Some contend that the only impact of interest rates is the direct cost of borrowing, since higher rates reduce corporate earnings and make it more expensive for consumers to purchase anything on credit. While it is true that the effective cost of anything from a new flat screen to a car to a house becomes more expensive or less expensive (if you borrow to make the purchase) based on rising or falling rates, impact of interest rates is much more far reaching.

If the equity risk premium (ERP) were a constant, cost of capital should change only to the extent that changes in inflation change the risk-free rate. For example, if inflation increased from 3 percent to 5 percent, then the risk-free rate should increase from 5 percent to 7 percent. Since earnings would be expected to increase with inflation by also growing 2 percent faster for the market as a whole, in the constant growth equation, where $P = E/(C - G)$ because C and G increase the same amount, the impact would be zero.

The RPF Model reveals the true impact. Since the ERP is proportionate to the risk-free rate, the cost of capital rises faster than the growth in earnings, causing decline in valuations. For example, using the RPF Model, where $C = R_f + R_f \times RPF$ and RPF equals 1.48, we can see that if R_f increases by 2 percent, then C increases by about 5 percent (2 percent + 2 percent × 1.48). Because G increases by only 2 percent, we end up with a net increase of 3 percent in the denominator, so P declines. Of course, it works the opposite way as well, if inflation falls by 2 percent, then C declines by 5 percent more than offsetting the decrease in growth, and prices rise. So in addition to the direct impact that interest rates have on earnings, they also have a large impact on price-to-earnings (P/E) multiples.

The S&P 500 peak month-end was October 2007, when it closed at 1,549, while the peak year-end risk-free rate was 1981, when the 10-year Treasury yield ended the year at 13.7 percent. Between these two mileposts, the S&P 500 Index increased 1.26× from 122 to 1,549, yet during the same period S&P operating earnings increased only 5.88×, rising from 15.2 to 89.3. If all variables other than earnings are held constant, then price would increase in direct proportion to E, so the index would have increase by only 5.88×. Since we know that the index increased by 1,264 percent, proportionately earnings account for only 47 percent (5. 88/1.264) of the growth, leaving the remaining increase to be explained by changes in the cost of capital. The RPF increased from 0.9 to 1.48 (see Chapter 2) and the 10-year Treasury yields fell to 4.47 percent in October 2007, driving the cost of capital from 26.1 percent down to 11.1 percent. Because earnings explain only 47 percent of the appreciation over the past 29 years, the remaining 53 percent is explained by changes to the RPF and risk-free rate.

As discussed in the Preface, many people consider the changes in P/E multiples that drove boom and bust markets since the 1960s to be unexplained. The RPF Model suggests that changes in interest rates are the missing piece that explains the variation.

EFFICIENT MARKET HYPOTHESIS

The RPF Model can help demystify valuation and also help explain major market events over the past 20-plus years. The exploration of these events sheds some light on the efficient market hypothesis (EMH). The EMH was first fully proposed by Eugene Fama in his doctoral thesis at the University of Chicago in the 1960s. In short, it states that the markets are "informationally efficient" in the sense that all available information is incorporated in the current stock price. The implication is that because all information is embodied in the current price, it should be impossible to beat the market.

Over time, it has been much debated and variations have emerged that allow for public, but not private, information (i.e., management) being incorporated in the current price or allow that it does not hold for small stocks that are not heavily traded. The EMH has been criticized, particularly by professional money managers, who would be out of work if the market were perfectly efficient (if you can't beat the market, why pay a professional manager—just buy index funds). Many people take the EMH to mean that the markets are always right. Today, even Fama admits the market makes mistakes: "In a period of high uncertainty, it's very difficult to figure out what the right prices are for stocks."[1]

Kenneth R. French a frequent collaborator with Fama, and a professor at the Tuck School of Business at Dartmouth, said in an interview jointly conducted with Fama that:

> *The efficient market hypothesis is just a model and, like all inter-esting models, it is not literally true. There are mistakes in prices even if one considers just publicly available information and, since people use financial prices to help decide how to allocate resources, those mistakes must affect the underlying reality. Of course, the existence of mistakes does not imply they are easy to find."[2]*

The RPF Model is a tool that can help find these mistakes.

HOW THE RPF VALUATION MODEL EXPLAINS BLACK MONDAY

U.S. and global markets plunged on October 19, 1987, with the S&P 500 declining more than 20 percent. The cause of the decline has been much discussed, with program trading often cited as the main culprit, along with portfolio insurance (derivatives).[3] The application of the RPF Model to this period is very revealing. Figure 4.1 shows actual versus predicted S&P levels, and Figure 4.2 shows actual versus predicted P/E ratios, along with Treasury yields. As shown, interest rates began climbing in March 1987, rising from 7.25 percent in March to 9.25 percent in October, driving down the predicted P/E and the predicted level of the S&P 500.[4] Yet, despite earnings remaining flat, the market grew by 12 percent from February to September (and a total of 25 percent from December). With the market crash in October, the predicted and actual fell back into parity, creating a clear outline of a bubble in both charts.

The suggestion offered by using the RPF Model to analyze events is that the underlying cause of the crash was excessive valuation relative to the sharp rise in interest rates. While actual and predicted levels often deviate, without a shift in the RPF, they tend to fall back in line.

Why did the market fall on October 19 and not November 19? The market began its decline in August. During the days before October 19, Iran had attacked a U.S flagged tanker, exacerbating fears that oil prices would continue to rise.[5] Perhaps this solidified the belief that earnings would not

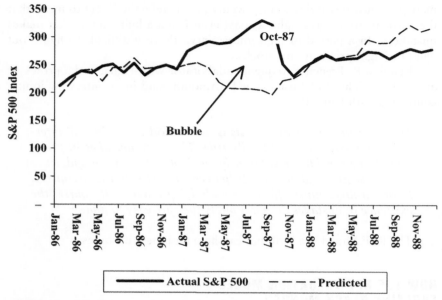

FIGURE 4.1 Actual versus Predicted during October 1987 Crash
Source: S&P earnings and price from 1988 to present from Standard & Poor's web site (www.standardandpoors.com/indices/sp-500/en/us/?indexId=spusa-500-usduf–p-us-l–); S&P monthly earnings for 1/86 to 11/88 from "Online Data Robert Shiller") www.econ.yale.edu/-shiller/data.htm); Treasury yields from Federal Reserve, H.15 Selected Interest Rates (www.federalreserve.gov/datadownload/Choose.aspx?rel=H.15). Because earnings are released quarterly, the model was extended to monthly and daily price data by using operating earnings as a constant for each month in the quarter applied for the month preceding quarter end (i.e., December to February = Q1) under the assumption that market expectations would have incorporated earning expectations.

rise and inflation would stay high, keeping interest rates high, and this point of view was rapidly assimilated into the market. I believe these were nothing more than the pin popping the balloon or a tipping point—actions that, while not particularly momentous, finally caused an unbalanced state to rapidly return to equilibrium—popping the bubble. While derivatives and program trading may have caused the market to fall rapidly after the descent began, they do not appear to have been the cause, just part of the mechanism allowing for the return to equilibrium. It is important to note that while you can identify a bubble, it might be impossible to anticipate or time events that cause it to pop.

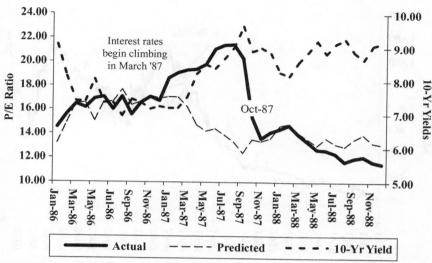

FIGURE 4.2 Interest Rate Impact on October 1987 Crash
Source: S&P earnings and price from 1988 to present from Standard & Poor's web
site (www.standardandpoors.com/indices/sp-500/en/us/?indexId=spusa-500-
usduf–p-us-l–); S&P monthly earnings for 1/86 to 11/88 from "Online Data Robert
Shiller" (www.econ.yale.edu/-shiller/data.htm); Treasury yields from Federal
Reserve, H.15 Selected Interest Rates (www.federalreserve.gov/datadownload/
Choose.aspx?rel=H.15). Because earnings are released quarterly, the model was
extended to monthly and daily price data by using operating earnings as a constant
for each month in the quarter applied for the month preceding quarter end (i.e.,
December to February = Q1) under the assumption that market expectations
would have incorporated earning expectations.

2000 "DOT-COM" BUBBLE: RPF MODEL SUGGESTS SIGNIFICANT BUBBLE FOR THE S&P 500

The National Association of Securities Dealers Automated Quotation
system (NASDAQ) peaked on March 10, 2000, at 5,132 in what is widely
considered to be a bubble driven by excessive valuations of Internet and
other technology companies. Many economists such as Robert Shiller,
author of *Irrational Exuberance*, believed that the entire market was
embroiled in a speculative bubble throughout this period.[6] Application of
the RPF Model to the S&P 500 strongly suggests that a significant bubble
did exist. Figure 4.3 shows the period from 1986 to December 2009. The
dot-com bubble appears as the greatest and most enduring bubble of the
entire period. Since it would be inappropriate to assume that the long-term

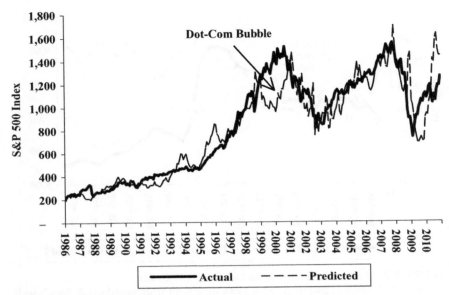

FIGURE 4.3   Actual versus Predicted during 2000 dot-com Bubble
Source: S&P earnings and price from 1988 to present from Standard & Poor's web
site (www.standardandpoors.com/indices/sp-500/en/us/?indexId=spusa-500-
usduf–p-us-l–); S&P Monthly earnings for 1/86 to 11/88 from "Online Data Robert
Shiller" (www.econ.yale.edu/-shiller/data.htm); Treasury yields from Federal
Reserve, H.15 Selected Interest Rates (www.federalreserve.gov/datadownload/
Choose.aspx?rel=H.15). Because earnings are released quarterly, the model was
extended to monthly and daily price data by using operating earnings as a constant
for each month in the quarter applied for the month preceding quarter end (i.e.,
December to February = Q1) under the assumption that market expectations
would have incorporated earning expectations.

growth of the smaller cap and technology-heavy NASDAQ would equal
long-term gross domestic product (GDP) growth and that volatility (beta)
would be the same as the S&P 500, the model was not applied to the
NASDAQ. Figure 4.4 illustrates the rise and fall of the NASDAQ Composite
Index during this period. From its March 10, 2000 high, the NASDAQ
had declined by 32 percent in mid-April and 51 percent by year-end
2000.

Prior to the fall, 10-year Treasury yields increased from 4.6 percent in
November 1998 to 6.2 percent in March 2000. While the NASDAQ began
to run up in late 1999, the S&P 500 Index began to diverge from RPF Model
predictions in January 1999.

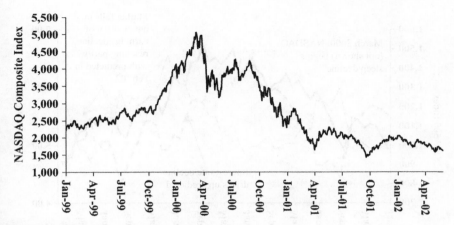

FIGURE 4.4   NASDAQ January 1999 to May 2002
Source: Yahoo Finance.

Figure 4.5 illustrates how the S&P 500 Index did not begin its decline until August 2000. (Remember, the model is applied using actual reported operating earnings, so predicted levels at any point are backward looking and do not reflect expectations.) However, the market began to anticipate that NASDAQ meltdown would have a negative impact on earnings and the index followed. Earnings fell by 27 percent from March 2000 to December 2001. The RPF Model would appear to have effectively signaled the expectation that earnings would fall well in advance of the actual reported drop.

The implication, then, is that the bubble was created by the combination of inflated earnings levels with rising 10-year Treasury yields that the market was somehow slow to recognize. To the extent the increases in interest rates were orchestrated by the Fed to cool an overheating economy, investors may have misread the signal and expected the increase in interest rates to be temporary. But as the rate increases began to affect earnings, the market began a sharp repricing as the new point of view was assimilated.

HOW THE RPF VALUATION MODEL EXPLAINS THE 2008 TO 2009 MELTDOWN AND RECOVERY

The bursting housing bubble and mortgage crisis ultimately led to the meltdown that began in September 2008. By August 2008, the S&P 500 had already fallen by 16 percent from its May 2007 peak. During this period,

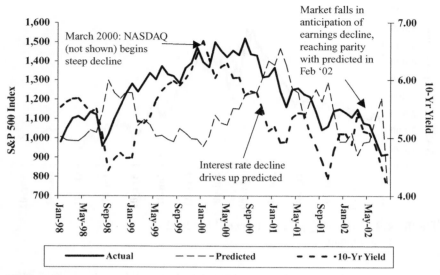

FIGURE 4.5 Dot-com Bubble Close Up
Source: S&P earnings and price from 1988 to present from Standard & Poor's web site (www.standardandpoors.com/indices/sp-500/en/us/?indexId=spusa-500-usduf–p-us-l–); Treasury Yields from Federal Reserve, H.15 Selected Interest Rates (www.federalreserve.gov/datadownload/Choose.aspx?rel=H.15). Because earnings are released quarterly, the model was extended to monthly and daily price data by using operating earnings as a constant for each month in the quarter applied for the month preceding quarter end (i.e., December to February = Q1) under the assumption that market expectations would have incorporated earning expectations.

10-year Treasury yields declined from around 5 percent to less than 4 percent. As illustrated in the chart below, this led to an increase in predicted levels of the S&P 500 index.

According to the Case-Schiller Home Price Index, home prices fell more than 10 percent from the second quarter of 2006 to the fourth quarter of 2007 and a total of 18 percent by the second quarter of 2008.[7] This historically large decline led to (well-founded) concerns of financial instability and eliminated an important source of disposable income. Once again, in anticipation of a decline in earnings, the S&P 500 Index fell while the RPF Model (using reported operating earnings) showed an increase in predicted levels as interest rates declined. The two lines begin to converge in August 2008, just before the worst of meltdown began in September and October. Investors were unable to absorb the seriousness of the pending crisis, so

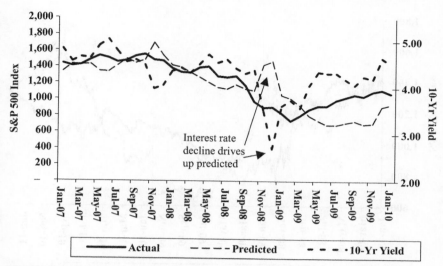

FIGURE 4.6 Actual versus Predicted and R_f (Monthly) during 2008 to 2009 Meltdown

Source: S&P earnings and price from 1988 to present from Standard & Poor's web site (www.standardandpoors.com/indices/sp-500/en/us/?indexId=spusa-500-usduf–p-us-l–); S&P monthly earnings for 1/86 to 11/88 from "Online Data Robert Shiller" (www.econ.yale.edu/-shiller/data.htm); Treasury yields from Federal Reserve, H.15 Selected Interest Rates (www.federalreserve.gov/datadownload/Choose.aspx?rel=H.15). Because earnings are released quarterly, the model was extended to monthly and daily price data by using operating earnings as a constant for each month in the quarter applied for the month preceding quarter end (i.e., December to February = Q1) under the assumption that market expectations would have incorporated earning expectations.

while the market fell in anticipation of earning declining, expectations did not come close to reflecting the magnitude of the situation.

Figure 4.6 shows actual levels of the S&P 500 along with levels predicted by the RPF Valuation Model and 10 Year Treasury Yields. The impact of abnormal interest rates is very evident with the predicted value climbing sharply as yields fell. It is important to keep in mind that not only should normalized inputs be used in the model, but they should also reflect long-term expectations. This is most true for earnings, but as seen here, also occasionally true for interest rates.

Figure 4.7 shows 2008 through early 2011 on a daily basis to further illustrate the predicted and actual price movements. Note that for daily charts, earnings are still changed only on a quarterly basis; changes in predicted reflect interest rate impact alone.

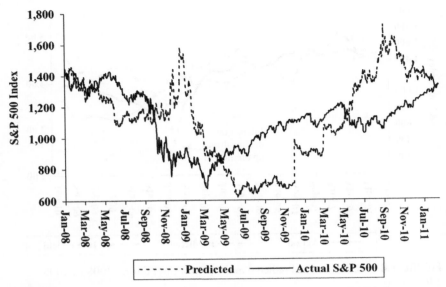

FIGURE 4.7 Actual versus Predicted (Daily) during 2008 to 2009 Meltdown
Source: S&P earnings and price from 1988 to present from Standard & Poor's web site (www.standardandpoors.com/indices/sp-500/en/us/?indexId=spusa-500-usduf–p-us-l–); S&P monthly earnings for 1/86 to 11/88 from "Online Data Robert Shiller" (www.econ.yale.edu/~shiller/data.htm); Treasury yields from Federal Reserve, H.15 Selected Interest Rates (www.federalreserve.gov/datadownload/Choose.aspx?rel=H.15). Because earnings are released quarterly, the model was extended to monthly and daily price data by using operating earnings as a constant for each month in the quarter applied for the month preceding quarter end (i.e., December to February = Q1) under the assumption that market expectations would have incorporated earning expectations.

The drop in interest rates clearly drives up the predicted levels, but as interest rates return to a more normal level by June 2009, predicted and actual return to parity.

MARKETS MOSTLY EFFICIENT AND RATIONAL, BUT PRONE TO MISTAKES

Analysis of these major market events with the RPF Model supports the contention that markets make mistakes in processing information. It also suggests that market prices oscillate around a true fair value price. At times, these deviations are very large. This was highlighted throughout this discussion of three major market events.

Over a longer period of time, the market is efficient if one allows for oscillations around true value, but is also subject to making mistakes, which can create bubbles. Over time, the bubbles are deflated and the market returns to predicted levels as new long-term views are assimilated. The RPF Valuation Model has shown to be useful in identifying bubbles before they pop.

This supports the contention that the valuation model worked well during this period with a normalized interest rate. It also shows how the market led predicted levels as it incorporated expected rather than actual historical operating earnings.

CHAPTER RECAP

Half of the growth in the S&P 500 Index since 1981 can be attributed to the cost of capital with risk-free rate declining from its peak of 13.7 percent in 1981. Interest rates were also the main culprit in the October 1987, where the market ignored rising interest rates and kept climbing, leading to creation of a significant bubble. The market crash collapsed the bubble with the predicted and actual falling back into parity.

The 2000 "dot-com" bubble was created by the combination of inflated earnings levels with rising 10-year Treasury yields that the market was slow to recognize. But as the rate increases began to affect earnings, the market began a sharp repricing as the new point of view was assimilated.

Perhaps surprisingly, during the 2008 to 2009 meltdown and recovery, predicted values for the model tracked actual throughout the crisis once earning expectations and unusually low Treasury yields are accounted for.

In sum, analysis of these major market events with the RPF Model supports the contention that markets make mistakes in processing information and pricing. It also suggests that market prices oscillate around a true fair value price and, as highlighted throughout this discussion of three major market events, these deviations can be very large. The model is useful in identifying these mistakes.

Applying the Risk Premium Factor Valuation Model

CHAPTER 5

Application to Market Valuation

The Risk Premium Factor (RPF) Model shows that the market is driven by three things: earnings, growth, and interest rates. Interest rates are the major driver of change in market price-to-earnings (P/E) ratios. The RPF Model makes it easy to test various future scenarios such as the impact of changes in inflation or earnings. Growth drives value, but not all sources of growth are equal. Earnings increases driven by revenue imply that a company can sustain long-term growth and are much more valuable than earnings driven by cost reduction. Top-line growth that drives earnings can lead to P/E multiple expansion. The RPF Model makes it easy to understand why.

Many people look at the market and valuation as a black box driven by emotion, leaving many managers unsure what strategies they can pursue to increase shareholder value. This section discusses the lessons that managers can draw from this simple model and apply it toward correcting some common misconceptions concerning market valuation. First let's reexamine the constant growth equation and the RPF Model:

$$P = E/(C - G)$$

$$P = E/((R_f \times (1 + RPF) - (R_f - Int_R + G_R))$$

This tells us that only three things matter:

1. Earnings.
2. Growth.
3. Interest rates, which drive cost of capital and embody real interest rates.

TABLE 5.1   Interest Rate Impact on Market P/E

Inputs							Output	
Variable	Constant				Calculated			
Risk-Free Rate (R_f)	Real Int. Rate%	RPF	Real Growth %	ERP %	Long-Term Inflation %	G %	Pred. PE	% Chg from Base
4.0%	2.0%	1.48	2.6%	5.9%	2.0%	4.6%	18.8	0%
6.0%	2.0%	1.48	2.6%	8.9%	4.0%	6.6%	12.1	−36%
8.0%	2.0%	1.48	2.6%	11.8%	6.0%	8.6%	8.9	−53%
10.0%	2.0%	1.48	2.6%	14.8%	8.0%	10.6%	7.0	−63%

P (valuation) will increase or decrease in direct proportion to E (earnings), and changes in interest rates have the inverse impact—rising interest rates reduce value, and falling interest rates increase value. For example, Table 5.1 shows that if yields on long-term Treasuries (R_f) rose from 4 percent to 6 percent, it would be expected to cause a 36 percent decline in valuation, while yields rising from 4 percent to 8 percent result in a 53 percent decline. The lesson: pay attention to inflation and watch the Treasury market!

Notice that as the risk-free rate increases, real growth and real interest rate remain constant, while inflation increases, resulting in an increase in G, the equity risk premium (ERP) also increases because it equals RPF times the risk-free rate, resulting in significantly lower P/E ratios.

There is very little value in making judgments about the market based on the long-run average P/E ratio. Some theorists claim that the market is overvalued just because P/E ratios are above historical average. You cannot make this judgment without putting P/Es in context of Treasury yields. P/E ratios do regress to a mean, but that mean is determined by the RPF Model.

BEWARE OF INTEREST RATES

It is well understood that interest rates impact cost of capital, but the RPF Model suggests that interest rate impact on cost of capital and by extension, valuation, is much greater than generally believed. Table 5.2 illustrates cost of capital (C) and P/E for a range of interest rates (R_f), using the RPF of 1.48, compared to employing a constant ERP of 7 percent.

In the constant ERP case, growth (G) increases in lockstep with interest rates (R_f), nullifying any impact of interest rate on valuation (P/E). The RPF model produces higher valuations at low interest rates, but at higher rates

TABLE 5.2 Constant ERP Implies Fixed P/E

	10-Year Rate% (R_f)	RPF	ERP	G	C	Pred. P/E
Constant ERP	4.00	—	7%	5%	11%	15.6
	5.00	—	7%	6%	12%	15.6
	6.00	—	7%	7%	13%	15.6
	8.00	—	7%	9%	15%	15.6
	10.00	—	7%	11%	17%	15.6
	12.00	—	7%	13%	19%	15.6
Risk Premium Factor	4.00	1.48	6%	5%	10%	18.8
	5.00	1.48	7%	6%	12%	14.7
	6.00	1.48	9%	7%	15%	12.1
	8.00	1.48	12%	9%	20%	8.9
	10.00	1.48	15%	11%	25%	7.0
	12.00	1.48	18%	13%	30%	5.8

valuations drop rapidly as cost of capital rises. This further illustrates the point that the long declines in interest rates beginning in 1981 were a major contributor to the long bull market. It also suggests caution in that the prospect of above normal returns fades as interest rates approach a floor.

EXAMPLE: APPLICATION TO THE MARKET IN LATE SEPTEMBER 2009

The Standard & Poor's (S&P) 500 closed the quarter ending September 30, 2009, at 1,057. The RPF Model predicted 745 (30 percent below actual) based on the following assumptions:

E = 39.61 based on S&P's estimate for the four quarters ending September 30, 2009.

R_f = 4.0 percent based on closing yields on 30-year Treasury (actually 4.05% but rounded down to simplify the illustration).

RPF = 1.48.

On the face of it, this seems to imply that the S&P was overvalued, which provides an opportunity to dig deeper and understand the results. The RPF Model allows an analyst to perform very simple "what ifs" using a combination of interest rates and earnings to develop an informed view of the market. If you believed the worst was over for corporate earnings and interest rates would remain low, perhaps there was a buying opportunity.

TABLE 5.3 TTM S&P 500 Operating—Q3 2009

Quarter Ending	Operating Earnings
09/30/2009	$15.78
06/30/2009	$13.81
03/31/2009	$10.11
12/31/2008	−$ 0.09
Total	$39.61

Source: Standard & Poor's.

There was reason to believe that the trailing 12-month (TTM) earnings at the end of September were not representative. Table 5.3 shows the composition of the $39.61.

The last quarter of 2008 was an earnings disaster, with the S&P 500 Index losing $0.09 per share in operating earnings. Fortunately, the loss was short-lived, with earnings recovering rapidly. If we were to assume that a more reasonable approximation of earnings and basis for valuation would be to project earnings for the full year 2009 by assuming the fourth quarter of 2009 would be at least as strong as the third quarter, then our input for earnings rises to $55.48 (39.61 + 0.09 + 15.78). This raises the predicted value for the index to 1,043, just 1.4 percent below actual. I make it a point not to dress up my charts by substituting data that fit the theory, preferring instead to highlight the differences and then discussing the deviations. In this case, it highlights the fact that the market appears to have expected earnings to recover.

TABLE 5.4 Meltdown and Recovery

	Inputs					Calculated			Output	
	30-Year Rate %	Earnings	Real Int. Rate %	RPF	Real G %	ERP %	Inflation %	G %	Pred. PE	Pred. S&P 500 Index
Trough Earnings	4.00	39.61	2.00	1.48	2.6	5.92	2.00	4.6	18.8	745
2009 Projected	4.00	55.48	2.00	1.48	2.6	5.92	2.00	4.6	18.8	1,043
Return to 2006/07	4.00	90.00	2.00	1.48	2.6	5.92	2.00	4.6	18.8	1,692
Earnings	5.00	90.00	2.00	1.48	2.6	7.40	3.00	5.6	14.7	1,324

Looking back to March 2009, when it was not at all clear that earnings would sustain a recovery, the predicted level based on earnings around $39 actually fit with a predicted value of 749, close to market bottom-out at 679 on March 9, 2009. Table 5.4 illustrates this, along with a look ahead. The model implied that if Treasury yields remained in the low 4 to 5 percent range and earnings recovered to 2007 levels, the market could stage a rally and recover to record levels. With S&P 500 earnings at $90 and Treasury yields of 4 percent, the model predicted an index level of 1,692 dropping to 1,324 with Treasury yields of 5 percent.

WHY THE SOURCE OF GROWTH MATTERS

All other variables being equal, investors will reward increased earnings, but only if they believe they are sustainable and, even better, the company can grow over the long term. Applying the RPF Model to valuation of an individual company is problematic because real growth cannot be assumed equal to long-term gross domestic product (GDP) as it does for the overall market. In order to account for the unique growth prospects of an individual company, valuation requires a discounted cash flow model over some time horizon. Cost of capital must also reflect an appropriate beta for the company. These concepts will be discussed in much more detail in later chapters. In this chapter, we want to explore the impact of long-term growth at the 20,000-foot level.

At this point you should have an understanding of the constant growth equation and, hopefully, believe it explains value in the market. In order to simplify this discussion, we will assume the long-term real growth (G) in the equation considers both short- and long-term growth prospects to arrive at a long-term average.

Valuation is not strictly formulaic in that variables are dynamic. Investors analyzing a company develop their own views on expected growth, so growing short-term earnings at the expense of expected long-term growth will lower valuation. While investors want to see earnings grow, they need to believe that both current earnings and growth rate are sustainable. The following example explores the impact of three different strategies on a company with a 10% cost of capital and current earnings of $100 million. Table 5.5 shows the impact of three strategies on value as evaluated using the constant growth equation, $P = E / (C - G)$. The strategies are:

- **Status quo.** Current earnings base growing at a real rate of 2 percent plus inflation.

TABLE 5.5 Impact of Growth Expenses on Valuation

	Inputs			Output		
Scenario	Earnings $M	Expected Long-Term Real Growth	Long-Term Inflation %	Total Growth (G)	Valuation $M @10%	% Chg from Base
Status Quo	100	2.0%	2.0%	4.0%	1,667	0%
Reduce R&D	120	0.0%	2.0%	2.0%	1,500	−10%
Growth Investment	90	3.5%	2.0%	5.5%	2,000	20%

- **Cut R&D and other expenses.** Increase earnings by 20 percent at the expense of long-term growth, which declines to 0 percent, plus inflation.
- **Invest in growth.** Earnings decrease by 10 percent, but expectations of long-term growth increase to 3.5 percent.

In the reduced R&D case, investors expect that despite the immediate increase in earnings, long-term growth will be limited, resulting in an overall reduction in value of 10 percent. If their expectations for growth were worse and they did not expect earnings to keep up with inflation, valuation would decline even further. In the growth investment case, investors are convinced that despite the lowering of current earnings, the investment will result in increased growth prospects, resulting in an increase in valuation by 20 percent despite a 10 percent reduction in profit.

These are simple examples designed to illustrate that valuation sometimes behaves in counterintuitive ways. Investors do not always punish reductions in earnings—it depends how they view the prospect for growth. The ability to communicate your story and demonstrate growth is critical. For example, assume two companies show annual earnings growth of 20 percent in the current year. The first company grows earnings by 20 percent but does not grow revenue. The second grows earnings by 20 percent and revenues by 10 percent. (*Note:* This is for illustration purposes. Ten percent revenue growth does not automatically equate to any specific long-term growth in earnings.) It would be reasonable for investors to expect that the first company cannot keep cutting expenses in perpetuity and will discount the achievement in earnings growth, while the second company, by demonstrating top-line growth, will be valued at a higher multiple, despite growing its annual earnings at the same rate.

TABLE 5.6 Cost Cuts vs. Top-Line Growth

		Inputs			Output	
Scenario	Earnings $M	Proj. Long-Term Real Growth	Long-Term Inflation %	Total Growth (G)	Valuation $M @10%	PE
Company 1:						
Cut Expenses	100	0.0%	2.0%	2.0%	1,250	12.5
Company 2:						
Grow Top Line	100	3.0%	2.0%	5.0%	2,000	20.0

Table 5.6 shows that Company 2 is worth 60 percent more than Company 1 because of growth expectations and thus trades at a P/E of 20 versus 12.5. When a company demonstrates that it can sustain earnings growth by growing revenue, its valuation multiple increases—also called *multiple expansion.*

The unfortunate reality is that the market does not always provide an immediate reward for making the right decisions and may even reward shortsightedness. While it is important to focus shareholder communication clearly on the growth story, showing a record of success is the sure way of creating value. One of the reasons private equity firms are believed to be so successful is that they can ignore fluctuations in quarterly earnings and focus on optimizing portfolio companies for attractive valuations on exit, while rewarding managers for driving sustainable growth.

CHAPTER RECAP

The stock market is driven by earnings, interest rates, and growth expectations. The RPF Model makes it easy to illustrate the impact of these factors on value. Rising interest rates are much more punishing to valuation than has been generally recognized—inflation is the enemy of valuation. The 2008 to 2009 meltdown was largely earnings driven. The strong market recovery in 2009 to 2010 was anticipated by the RPF Model, using reasonable forward assumptions.

This chapter contains one of the most important messages for corporate executives—all sources of earnings growth are not equal. Increasing your P/E multiple requires demonstrated ability to drive sustainable growth. In tough times, growth initiatives are often slashed because they rarely produce results in the current year. And, in fact, with no way of knowing whether these initiatives will produce growth, the market will often reward the cost-cutting decision—over the short term. Driving value requires a focus on long-term growth.

Remember:

- Higher growth rates result in higher P/E multiples.
- Multiple expansion occurs when investors believe growth rates have increased (assuming constant cost of capital).

CHAPTER 6

Risk-Adjusted Real Implied Growth Rate (RIGR)

The Risk Premium Factor (RPF) Model can be used to solve for implied values of any variable based on current valuations. This analysis is useful for understanding the overall market and individual companies.

In addition to assessing the stock market's current value versus predicted, the RPF Model can be used to extract implied values for any of its variables by rearranging the equation, $P = E/(R_f \times (1 + RPF) - (R_f - Int_R + G_R))$, to solve for the implied value of any variable:

$$\text{Real Growth } (G_R) = (R_f \times (1 + RPF) - (R_f - Int_R)) - E/P$$

$$\text{Risk-Free Rate } (R_f) = (E/P - Int_R + G_R)/RPF$$

$$RPF = (E/P - Int_R + G_R)/R_f$$

$$\text{Earnings } (E) = P \times (R_f \times (1 + RPF) - (R_f - Int_R + G_R))$$

Note that since the original equation is obviously not valid for earnings (E) of less than zero or for values approaching zero, none of these equations should be used where E is negative or very low.

These transformations have multiple direct uses. With confidence in one or more observed variables, the equations can be used to test hypotheses, such as solving for the implied growth rate at a given current price, then testing those results at different interest rate levels. For example, on October 10, 2010, the 30-year yield was 3.7 percent, forward earnings were $80, and the Standard & Poor's (S&P) Index was 1,163, so the implied long-term real growth rate was only 0.6 percent. Bear in mind that is not next year's growth but in perpetuity. It is hard to believe that the long-term growth rate for the

S&P 500, which should parallel the overall economy, should be less than 1 percent. The clear implication is that something is misaligned. Bonds could be in a bubble, earnings could fall, the market could rise, or perhaps the RPF has shifted. Using standard assumptions, the implied yield on the 30-year (risk-free rate) was 5.1 percent.

ANALYZING INDIVIDUAL COMPANIES WITH RIGR

Using the RPF Model to determine the stock price for an individual company is not practical, simply because it's impossible to derive the long-term growth rate necessary to derive valuation without creating a multiyear projection, however, the model is useful in deriving market expectations. In other words, based on the current share price, how fast does the market expect earnings to grow or shrink? Real implied growth rate (RIGR) shows the market expectations for long-term growth implied in an individual firm's stock price. Comparing RIGR for a single firm to the overall market and its industry can help investors indentify over- and undervalued firms and sectors.

In the preceding example, we found that on October 11, 2010, the implied real growth for the market was only 0.6 percent. As discussed earlier, this seems very low. While there is no way to be sure, it does not really matter if we are making relative comparisons. The real question is, how do a company's growth expectations compare to its peers and the entire S&P 500?

According to the Capital Asset Pricing Model (CAPM), Cost of Equity $= R_f + \beta \times$ Equity Risk Premium (ERP). We know that by definition the beta (β) for the entire market is 1.0. For convenience, this term is usually left out of the RPF Model when evaluating the entire market. When evaluating individual companies we can insert β to derive the company risk premium. Under the RPF Model:

$$ERP = R_f \times RPF$$

So the company risk premium is simply $R_f, \times \beta \times RPF$. Therefore, to apply the RPF Model for an individual company, we only need to substitute $\beta \times RPF$ for RPF in the original equation.

$$P = E/(R_f \times (1 + RPF \times \beta) - (R_f - Int_R + G_R))$$

$$\text{Real Growth } (G_R) = (R_f \times (1 + RPF \times \beta) - (R_f - Int_R)) - E/P$$

This was applied to every company in the S&P 500 using data from I-Metrix. Because the model does not hold for negative and near-zero

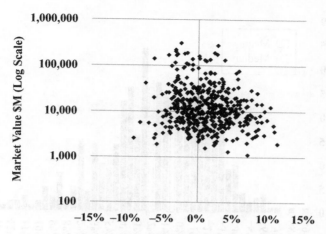

FIGURE 6.1   Real Implied Growth Rate (RIGR) Distribution
(October 7, 2010)
Source: I-Metrix data, author's analysis.

earnings, companies with negative earnings and high price-to-earnings (P/E) ratio (> 80) were eliminated, along with low P/E companies (< 5) as outliers.

Based on aggregate operating earnings for the S&P 500 Index, the expected growth was just 0.6 percent on October 7, 2010, but median real growth was 2.1 percent. Not surprisingly, the largest firms with the most earnings have lower growth expectations. Figure 6.1 shows real growth expectations plotted against market value.

You can see the concentration of large-market-cap companies with growth rates below zero (upper left quadrant), explaining why the median growth rate is higher than the aggregate implied growth for the index.

It is important to note that since no other adjustments were made to individual companies' results before calculating RIGR, individual company results need to be examined closely. For example, as will be discussed later, individual company RIGR might be adjusted for equity investments and high cash balances. These adjustments would give a better picture of the individual company.

Figure 6.2 shows the distribution risk-adjusted RIGR for firms in the S&P 500 on October 7, 2010. Figure 6.3 shows the distribution risk-adjusted RIGR for firms in the S&P 500 on December 31, 2010.

It's interesting to note the shift in RIGR between these two dates driven by the decline in yields coupled with the rise in the S&P 500 Index.

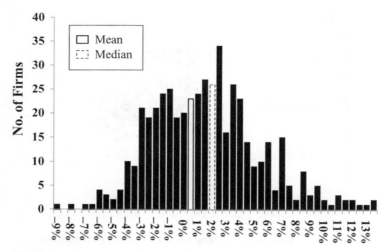

FIGURE 6.2   S&P 500 RIGR Distribution (October 7, 2010)
Source: I-Metrix data, author's analysis.

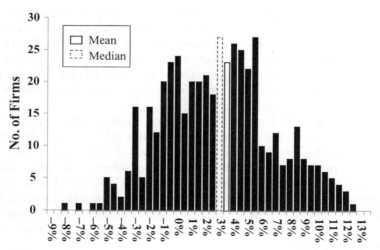

FIGURE 6.3   S&P 500 RIGR Distribution (December 31, 2010)
Source: I-Metrix data, author's analysis.

TABLE 6.1 Changes in Predicted, Actual, and RIGR in Late 2010

	28-Sep	31-Dec
30-year Treasury	3.7%	4.5%
Market RIGR	0.6%	1.8%
Median RIGR	1.3%	2.9%
Mean RIGR	1.7%	3.3%
S&P 500 Actual	1,147	1,267
S&P Predicted	1,641	1,437

Source: I-Metrix data, author's analysis.

Table 6.1 shows how the parameters changed as predicted and actual began to converge.

This can be seen Figures 6.2 and 6.3, where RIGR for the market shifted toward the right.

Because the current market levels may not always be reflective of expectations, it is useful to develop a normalized comparison by putting implied growth for individual firms in perspective compared to overall market. Evaluating RIGR for an individual firm requires putting it in context relative to its peers and the overall market. For example, on October 7, 2010, Microsoft had the following:

Consensus P/E estimate 10.39

$\beta = 0.81$

$R_f = 3.7\%$

$Int_R = 2.0\%$

$RPF = 1.48$

So implied real growth $= -2.9\%$ (even before adjusting for cash), implying that investors expect Microsoft to suffer a long-term decline in earnings. Is that reasonable? Obviously, it depends on your view of Microsoft's business. Since I don't have any special insights into Microsoft's operations, let's compare it to the rest of the U.S. software industry. Table 6.2 shows Microsoft compared to U.S. software companies as classified by Market Guide.

Not only does Microsoft rank near the bottom of the software industry in terms of growth, but near the bottom of the entire S&P 500. The percentile rank is just 11 percent, meaning the market expected 89 percent of the S&P 500 to grow faster than Microsoft.

TABLE 6.2   Computer Software Industry RIGR Analysis—October 7, 2010

Ticker	Name	Price	P/E TTM	P/E (Cnsens Est.)	Risk-Adj. Real Impl. Growth Rate (RIGR)	Pctile
ADBE	ADOBE INC	28.69	32.13	18.39	2.9%	63%
ADSK	AUTODESK	31.94	42.00	31.62	7.4%	96%
BMC	BMC	42.32	18.98	17.13	1.7%	48%
CA	CA, INC.	21.39	14.27	12.02	0.3%	35%
CPWR	COMPUWARE	8.63	19.78	17.61	2.8%	60%
CTSH	COGNIZANT	64.30	32.04	28.20	5.7%	87%
CTXS	CITRIX	60.46	47.30	41.70	5.6%	87%
ERTS	ELEC. ARTS	17.58	(16.47)	87.90	NA	NA
INTU	INTUIT INC	45.91	27.68	21.76	2.8%	61%
MFE	MCAFEE	47.15	44.54	23.11	1.5%	46%
MSFT	MICROSOFT	24.53	11.67	10.39	−2.8%	11%
NOVL	NOVELL INC	5.89	(10.18)	25.61	2.6%	59%
ORCL	ORACLE	27.69	22.08	14.57	0.5%	38%
RHT	RED HAT	38.17	53.18	66.96	7.4%	96%
SAI	SAIC, INC.	15.90	11.78	11.04	−3.8%	7%
SYMC	SYMANTEC	15.03	15.37	12.96	0.2%	34%
VRSN	VERISIGN	31.98	28.68	34.39	4.4%	79%
	Average				2.4%	57%

S&P 500 Median RIGR = 2.1%

S&P 500 Aggregate RIGR = 0.6%

Source: I-Metrix data, author's analysis.

This alone is not a reason to put Microsoft on your buy list, but it does call for deeper analysis and help formulate questions we might want to explore. Windows and Office make up the bulk of Microsoft revenues. Should we expect those products to go into long-term decline in volume and price? Will efforts in mobile and search continue to fail? Or will continued growth in computer power in the coming years increase the need for Microsoft's operating systems and tools to harness the power?

If Microsoft puts together a few quarters of revenue and earnings growth, will market expectations rise? Even bringing RIGR up to 0 percent, just growing with inflation would expand Microsoft's P/E multiple by perhaps 40 percent to about 15—some good upside. Evaluating real implied growth helps identify companies that may be mispriced relative to the market or its peers and suggests where further analysis can be leveraged. The next few sections describe an RIGR analysis of Apple and Google post-earnings.

TABLE 6.3 Computer Hardware RIGR Analysis—October 13, 2010

Ticker	Name	Price	P/E TTM	P/E (Cnsens Fcst)	Risk-Adj. Implied Real Growth Rate (RIGR)	Pctile
		Date:	10/13/2010			
APPL	APPLE	298.54	2.62	20.50	2.8%	67%
DELL	DELL INC	13.92	7.62	10.79	−0.9%	30%
HPQ	HEWLETT PACKARD	41.35	9.94	9.17	−3.7%	7%
LXK	LEXMARK	44.60	11.23	9.70	−1.5%	25%
EMC	EMC CORP	20.20	27.30	20.61	2.9%	68%
NTAP	NETAPP	48.77	40.31	30.11	6.0%	87%
SNDK	SANDISK	40.07	9.05	10.04	1.5%	52%
WDC	WESTERN DIGITAL	29.42	4.96	8.22	−2.1%	19%
	Average				0.6%	44%

Source: Data from I-Metrix (http://i-metrix.edgar-online.com/).

RIGR ANALYSIS OF APPLE AND GOOGLE PRE-EARNINGS ANNOUNCEMENT

This analysis is taken from an article that I published on the Seeking Alpha web site on October 14, 2010.[1] RIGR analysis showed growth expectations for both Google and Apple were in the upper 60th percentile for S&P 500 companies—closer to the middle than the top.

Tables 6.3 and 6.4 show RIGR for computer hardware and computer services industries as defined by Market Guide.

While we might reasonably place companies like Hewlett-Packard and IBM in the same industry, for consistency we will stick with the Market Guide industries.

- RIGR for Google and Apple are 2.6 percent and 2.8 percent putting them in the 65th and 67th percentile relative to the S&P 500—closer to the middle than the top.
- Hewlett-Packard and IBM both had negative RIGR, implying the market expected earnings of both to decline over time. They both ranked in the bottom 20 percent of the S&P 500 in terms of growth expectations.
- Yahoo, perhaps surprisingly to some, had RIGR of 2.4 percent, putting the company at the 64th percentile, close to Google and Apple in terms of growth expectations.

TABLE 6.4   Computer Services RIGR Analysis—October 13, 2010

Ticker	Name	Price	P/E TTM	P/E (Cnsen Fcst)	Risk-Adj. Implied Real Growth Rate (RIGR)	Pctile
		Date:	10/13/2010			
ADBE	AKAMAI	45.86	57.33	46.32	7.1%	91%
CERN	CERNER	85.53	33.94	31.22	4.4%	80%
CRM	SALESFORCE	105.47	191.76	159.80	9.3%	96%
CSC	CSC	47.01	8.90	8.87	−3.7%	7%
DNB	D&B	75.25	15.74	13.61	−1.6%	22%
FISV	FISERV	54.09	16.34	13.46	−0.4%	35%
GOOG	GOOGLE	541.39	23.55	22.20	2.6%	65%
IBM	IBM	139.85	12.94	12.40	−1.9%	21%
TDC	TERADATA	37.99	22.35	22.22	3.0%	68%
TSS	TOTAL SYS.	15.50	14.09	15.82	1.5%	52%
YHOO	YAHOO	14.43	21.54	20.61	2.4%	64%
	Average				2.0%	54%

Source: Data from I-Metrix (http://i-metrix.edgar-online.com/), author's analysis.

Why would Yahoo, a company many considered to be struggling, have similar expectations for growth to Google and Apple? First, we need to recognize that Yahoo's market value includes its stake in Alibaba Group, valued at $5 to $10 billion, but not contributing to earnings, so the market value relative is inflated relative to earnings. Putting this aside, the market is a dispassionate arbiter. While Google and Apple are truly exceptional companies, there is a real question as to whether they can sustain the current level of growth. Meanwhile, Yahoo, which has underperformed operationally and was under considerable pressure, might be viewed as a turnaround prospect.

Since valuation falls if expected growth declines, some of the key questions are:

- While Google dominated search advertising and has a pipeline of exciting products, can these new products generate sizable profits?
- The iPhone and iPad accounted for a significant chunk of Apple revenue. Could they maintain growth and margins in iPhone and iPad in the face of increasing competition?

Since this first pass was performed just prior to Apple and Google's quarterly earnings release, we were able to assess the impact of those announcements. Both companies had strong results, with Apple reporting earnings up 68 percent over the prior year, while Google reported earnings

TABLE 6.5 Computer Hardware RIGR Analysis—October 19, 2010

Ticker	Name	Price	P/E TTM	P/E (Cnsens Fcst)	Risk-Adj. Implied Real Growth Rate (RIGR)	Pctile
		Date:	10/13/2010			
APPL	APPLE	309.49	20.43	20.43	2.8%	67%
DELL	DELL INC	14.49	18.34	11.23	−0.5%	33%
HPQ	HEWLETT PACKARD	42.83	10.30	9.50	−3.3%	8%
LXK	LEXMARK	45.20	11.39	9.83	−1.3%	27%
EMC	EMC CORP	20.83	26.04	21.26	3.0%	68%
NTAP	NETAPP	51.00	42.15	31.48	6.2%	88%
SNDK	SANDISK	38.13	8.61	9.56	0.9%	46%
WDC	WESTERN DIGITAL	30.20	5.09	8.48	−1.6%	22%
	Average				0.8%	45%

Source: Data from I-Metrix (http://i-metrix.edgar-online.com/), author's analysis.

grew by 49 percent, excluding one-time charges. Tables 6.5 and 6.6 show RIGR for the same companies as earlier, with Google and Apple highlighted for comparison.

RIGR for Google and Apple were 3.1 percent and 2.8 percent, respectively, putting them in the 69th and 67th percentile relative to the S&P 500. This compared to the percentile rankings of 65 for Google and 67 for Apple, about a week prior, on October 13, 2010. I published a follow-up article showing that Google was now expected to grow faster than Apple.[2] Table 6.7 shows how the key factors changed post–earnings announcement.

Share price for both companies increased following their earnings releases. Forecast earnings for Apple actually increased more than the updated 2010 forecast for Google, yet RIGR was unchanged for Apple, while it rose significantly for Google. Given the higher current growth, why had growth expectations for Apple not risen more than Google?

RIGR measures long-term expected growth. Both companies exceeded expectations, even though expectations for Google's 2010 earnings did not increase as much as Apple's. Over the long term, investors expected Google to be able to sustain higher growth. The relative strength of competitive threats is a key consideration. While Apple was firing on all cylinders with earnings up 68 percent from the same quarter last year, competition to iPhone and iPad were likely to increase. Meanwhile, Google, while in a competitive business, had little new competition on the horizon. The impact of potential competition was heightened, with Apple reporting that gross margins fell. Apple's gross margins had fallen to 36.9 percent from

TABLE 6.6 Computer Services RIGR Analysis—October 19, 2010

Ticker	Name	Price	P/E TTM	P/E (Cnsen Fcst)	Risk-Adj. Implied Real Growth Rate (RIGR)	Pctile
		Date:	10/13/2010			
ADBE	AKAMAI	45.54	56.93	46.00	6.9%	91%
CERN	CERNER	85.16	33.79	31.08	4.5%	81%
CRM	SALESFORCE	103.63	188.42	157.02	9.2%	96%
CSC	CSC	48.95	9.27	9.24	−3.2%	9%
DNB	D&B	75.17	15.73	13.59	−1.6%	22%
FISV	FISERV	54.87	16.58	13.62	−0.3%	35%
GOOG	GOOGLE	607.83	24.69	24.15	3.1%	69%
IBM	IBM	138.03	12.22	12.24	−2.1%	19%
TDC	TERADATA	37.31	21.95	21.82	2.9%	67%
TSS	TOTAL SYS.	15.70	14.27	16.02	1.6%	53%
YHOO	YAHOO	15.49	23.12	22.13	2.8%	67%
	Average				2.1%	54%

Source: Data from I-Metrix (http://i-metrix.edgar-online.com/), author's analysis.

41.8 percent, and the company expected further declines. According to the *New York Times:*

> *Apple's profit margins are the envy of the consumer electronics industry. The problem was that the company's newest products ware not as profitable as its computers and iPod music players. Strong sales of lower-margin products—the iPad among them—caused the decline, according to Apple executives.*[3]

TABLE 6.7 Post-Earnings Change in RIGR

	Apple			Google		
	13-Oct-10	19-Oct-10	% Chg	13-Oct-10	19-Oct-10	% Chg
Share Price	298.54	309.49	3.7%	541.39	607.83	12.3%
EPS 2010 Fcst/Act	14.56	15.15	4.1%	24.39	25.17	3.2%
Forward P/E (2010)	20.50	20.43		22.20	24.15	
RIGR	2.8%	2.8%		2.6%	3.1%	
RIGR Pctile	67%	67%		65%	69%	

And from Market Watch:

"In the absence of high expectations, Apple's quarter would be viewed well," wrote Keith Bachman of BMO Capital Markets in a note to clients. "However, we believe investors will give an appropriate amount of focus on the relatively weak gross margins."[4]

The iPhone and iPad, responsible for the bulk of the growth, are lower margin than other Apple products, so increased competition to these products could further erode margins. RIGR shows that this concern was baked into Apple's stock price.

CHAPTER RECAP

RIGR analysis uses the RPF Model to calculate risk-adjusted real implied growth expectations implied in stock price. Because inflation is stripped out, RIGR can be compared across time periods. RIGR can be useful in understanding market expectations and developing a point of view on the expectations as an input for investing decisions. Comparing company RIGR to the overall market creates useful relative comparison that is not dependent on overall market valuation. Observed changes in company RIGR indicates changes in growth expectations and can provide useful insight into how the market views earnings and other announcements.

CHAPTER 7

Valuing an Acquisition or Project

Risk Premium Factor (RPF) modeling principles can be applied to acquisition or project evaluation to overcome common pitfalls in valuation. The most important applications are in determining cost of capital and using the model to calculate terminal value. This also requires setting a reasonable time horizon. Whether it is a merger-and-acquisition (M&A) transaction or upgrading a piece of equipment, the same principles apply. The RPF Model removes debate about the equity risk premium (ERP). Setting the investment horizon (length of your forecast) is critical to valuing a company or project, especially when using the RPF Model to determine terminal value. The time horizon needs to be developed relative the growth and cyclicality of the business under evaluation. The terminal value captures the value of your forecast beyond the horizon. While typically accounting for a large share of total value, it rarely receives the same diligence as the forecast within the horizon. The RPF Model helps establish a reasonable terminal value consistent with market valuation.

Countless books and articles have been written on the subjects of mergers and acquisitions and valuation. These next few chapters will outline only the highest-level basics with the dual purpose of providing a high-level overview of how to value a company or project to those unfamiliar with the practice, along with providing those familiar or even expert in valuation, a deeper dive into the application of the RPF Model to general discounted cash flow (DCF) valuation, including the calculation of cost of capital and determination of terminal value. Because calculating the terminal value requires a normalized cash flow to create a good result, a significant portion of the discussion in these chapters is focused on setting the appropriate time horizon, dealing with cyclicality and estimating long-term growth. The end goal is to give you some understanding of how to value a business and how to apply RPF Model concepts. In order to avoid diluting the important points related to the RPF Model, the discussion largely ignores many important factors, such as a detailed discussion of cash flow modeling, taxation, depreciation, goodwill, and other accounting concepts that have a significant impact on value and often drive deal structure. One should not attempt to construct their own analysis without proper grounding in these areas. For a deeper dive into the subject, I recommend *Valuation: Measuring and Managing the Value of Companies,* Fifth Edition (Wiley, 2011) by McKinsey's Tim Koller, Marc Goedhart, and David Wessels.

BRIEF INTRODUCTION TO VALUING AN ACQUISITION OR PROJECT

The value of a company or project is simply the present value of its future cash flows. The approach can be quite simple. Consider the example in Table 7.1.

The investment of $100 generates the revenue and cash flows as shown in Table 7.1. With a 10 percent cost of capital, the present value is $125. Subtracting the initial investment yields a net present value (NPV) of $25. So, if all goes well, the project is expected to create $25 in value above the initial investment.

TABLE 7.1 Basic DCF Example

	Year 1	Year 2	Year 3	Year 4	Year 5
Revenue	100	110	120	130	140
Cost	75	70	75	80	85
Depreciation	20	20	20	20	20
EBIT	5	20	25	30	35
Tax	2	8	10	12	14
Net Income	3	12	15	18	21
Add Back Depreciation	20	20	20	20	20
Operating Cash Flow	23	32	35	38	41
PV @ 10%	$125				
Investment	(100)				
Net Present Value	$25				

This begs three questions:

1. Why 10 percent?
2. What happens after year 5?
3. Why five years?

Let's take them one a time. *Why 10 percent?* The reality is that in some companies the cost of capital is set and forgotten, never to be changed, regardless of any changes to the outside world. In others, the cost of capital is calculated, but not adjusted with frequency and precision. The next chapter will cover my recommended approach.

What happens after year 5? This is called the terminal value. This is the value of the project beyond the forecast horizon, and it's hugely important. It will be discussed in detail later in this chapter.

Why five years? Five years is the project horizon. Presumably, in Table 7.1, the project is expected to have no value after five years. Since we don't have a terminal value, we are assuming it's zero. Project time horizons will be discussed later.

TRANSLATING YOUR WORLDVIEW INTO NUMBERS

Before continuing in our discussion of valuation, let's step back and think about why we are developing a forecast model in the first place. If you think of your model as some sort of separate thing composed of growth rates, margins, and a cost of capital, while losing sight of the big picture, your efforts are doomed. The most important function of a financial model is translating your worldview as it applies to your industry, target, or project, into a set of assumptions that can be used as inputs and tested for reasonableness. You should have noted that when we discussed the application of the model in previous chapters, the output was used to help understand the status quo, not make a free-standing determination.

Developing Your Worldview

Developing your worldview requires looking at the past in order to think about the future. The information you need to develop your worldview is usually at hand, but the pieces need to be assembled. I wrote two articles (included in the appendix material for this book) for SeekingAlpha.com that illustrates this point.

The first, "Mobile Apps: The Wave of the Past," published on September 28, 2010, took the position that despite the fact that mobile apps were undergoing tremendous growth at the time on iPhone and Android platforms, they were unlikely to maintain their hold on mobile in the future. I argued that rather than following its own path, mobile would repeat the pattern of growth seen in PCs. When PCs were introduced, they were 100 percent app machines (in that all the software resided on the computer) because there was only very limited connectivity in the form of dial-up time-share services. They were also slow and had small screens. As PC speeds increased and, most important, the Internet proliferated, then got fast, applications began migrating to the Web, replacing native apps. Early PC apps (AOL and Pointcast) were introduced to overcome the inherent slowness of early Internet connections by caching data. This fell out of use once Internet speeds increased. There did not seem to be any reason that this pattern would not repeat for mobile, which, of course, is still working to overcome small screens, slow processers, and spotty connections.

This view has some significant implications. Some device manufacturers, like Apple, benefit from a proprietary platform—the so-called walled garden. AOL was the original walled garden and suffered with the migration to the Web. Some players could lose that benefit as applications migrated from apps to the Web from proprietary platforms. Publishers who have heavily invested in apps should consider exit strategies to pave the migration to mobile Web.

Time will tell if I was right. The point here is not to argue the future of mobile but to illustrate the approach and thought process.

The second article, "Technology on the Horizon: What if Moore's Law Continues for Another 40 Years?," was published on SeekingAlpha.com on December 6, 2010. This article discusses the potential impact of Moore's Law continuing for the next 40 year. Moore's Law was originally articulated by Intel cofounder, Gordon Moore, who wrote an article for *Electronics* magazine in April 1965, describing his thesis that the number of transistors that can be placed on a chip will roughly double every two years. As it turns out, he was right, and that pace continued at least through 2010.

Since the other manifestation of Moore's Law is that price drops by 50 percent every two years for the same amount of computing power, the overall impact of the trend's continuing for another 40 years is profound. By 2020, the price of an iPhone equivalent would drop from about $600 to $18.75 and keep falling to $0.59 by 2030. Overall computing power and price would improve 1 million–fold by 2050. While it's entirely possible that the trend will not continue, if you are developing strategy for a technology company, how can you ignore the possibility?

In the article, I posed questions to consider:

- Where can very inexpensive but small and powerful computing be applied in the future?

- What capabilities could exist with more power that are not practical or at least just not good enough for primetime today?
- What products and services have good present potential but could be enormous if Moore's Law continues?

The underlying thought is: if Moore's Law continues, how can you profit? One way is to look for things that are already technically possible, just too expensive. Back in the late 1980s, people were already talking about video on demand and interactive television. Time Warner's first live trial was in 1994. As reported in the *New York Times*, "The point of the Orlando experiment, Time Warner executives say, is to find out what people will want when the equipment that is now so expensive becomes affordable several years down the road."[1]

How can you make money from this insight? Investing in cable operators or technology providers is one route. Another, and perhaps easier, is to look for the losers. Video chains like Blockbuster were destined to lose.

Most of today's hugely successful consumer electronic devices were available or publicly touted years ago. In 1993 and 1994 AT&T ran an advertising campaign with the tag lines, "Have you ever ..." and "You will." You can find it on YouTube by search for "AT&T You Will Ads." Tom Selleck narrates and asks questions like, "Have you ever borrowed a book from thousands of miles away (showing a student using a computer)? Crossed the country without stopping for directions (showing a GPS)?" It goes on to describe automatic toll lanes, Web cams, smart cards, videoconferencing, video on demand, tiny mobile phones, and distance learning. All of these things are mainstream today.

It's hard to imagine developing a strategy, investing, and acquiring without having articulated a view or set of scenarios about the future, especially in technology businesses.

MobAppCo Assumptions

Let's assume it is 2006 and we are trying to decide whether to acquire MobAppCo, a company that develops applications for mobile phones, an emerging business, for $10 million, and contrast two approaches:

1. The pure financial model approach
2. The worldview approach

In the pure financial model approach, we might estimate that we will sell 100,000 per month at a net profit of $2 each per month—revenues of $2.4 million per year. While it does produce a forecast, it tells us nothing about the business and what we need to succeed or what assumptions are key. In the worldview approach, we build a model based on the key drivers of this business and use it to help understand the impact of our key assumptions, such as:

- How many mobile devices will we be able to run on?
- How will this change over time?
- What are the global trends regarding mobile applications? Do we expect it to change?
- What is our marketing strategy? How will we promote the product, what is our customer acquisition cost, and what is our customer lifetime value?

We are not answering a series of questions dictated by our model, but building a model that is an expression of our strategy and industry analysis.

Using this approach, we first identify our worldview or investment thesis regarding these assumptions. First, recognize that it's 2006 and the iPhone has not been released and the app stores have not been introduced. Blackberry is the dominant smartphone, and the major carriers offer a variety of applications on feature phones as well as smartphones. Looking at the sales trends on Blackberry and other smartphones, combined with rapidly falling costs, we think that smartphones will proliferate widely and consumers will be receptive to new web sites and applications. We will establish relationships with major carriers and handset manufacturers to promote our applications, and based on initial conversations, we are confident we can establish these relationships.

We build our model focusing on revenues and distribution. First focusing on the number of addressable handsets, we develop a handset forecast. With rapidly falling costs, a respected industry analyst expects that 50 percent of handsets sold will meet our specification in just three years. Knowing that the average consumer keeps a handset for three years, we can develop a handset forecast (just to be clear, these figures are only for illustration) for the next five years.

Our application is designed for an outdoorsy group of people that represents 10 percent of the U.S. population. We assume that their handset purchase pattern is the same as the general population. We might also include projections for other factors like customer churn, but have left them out to keep this example simple. Table 7.2 shows our revenue projections.

We are least confident in our projection for the 1 percent sell-through rate because we were unable to find any comparable benchmarks. As we review the forecast, we know this is one of the keys to our valuation, and even at this rate, our application generates only $0.13 million in revenue in the first year.

TABLE 7.2 Revenue Model for MobAppCo

$ Millions	2006	2007	2008	2009	2010
Existing Number of Addressable					
Handsets	3.0	8.0	25.9	70.3	101.5
Number Handsets Sold in					
United States	100.0	103.0	106.1	109.3	112.6
% Addressable	6%	20%	50%	50%	50%
Total Addressable Sold	6.0	20.6	53.0	54.6	56.3
Addressable of Handsets Retired	(1.0)	(2.7)	(8.6)	(23.4)	(33.8)
Ending Addressable Handsets	8.0	25.9	70.3	101.5	124.0
Average Addressable Handsets	5.5	17.0	48.1	85.9	112.7
Target Market @ 10%	0.55	1.70	4.81	8.59	11.27
Sell-though Rate	1%	5%	1%	1%	1%
Avg. Customers	0.01	0.02	0.05	0.09	0.11
Rev. Customer/Month	$2.00	$2.00	$2.00	$2.00	$2.00
Annual Revenue	$0.13	$0.41	$1.16	$2.06	$2.71

The value of these projections goes beyond producing a financial forecast to helping provide a framework for discussing our strategy. The pure financial forecast seemed reasonable with the expectation to sell 100,000 subscribers out of millions of phones. But when we broke the forecast down based on our market analysis and strategy, we found that the project looked much less attractive.

Let's say the CEO was championing the deal. The model provides a structure for the potentially difficult conversation around killing his or her pet project. It makes it easy to lay out the case in a dispassionate and objective manner. Here is what we know and believe, and here are the things we are not sure about. Let's stipulate the facts and focus on the uncertainties, in this case, the sell-through rate. Since the sell-through rate has the least factual support, one approach is to reverse-engineer the question. In other words, determine what sell-through rate we need in order to achieve our financial targets. Let's assume that means we need $2 million in revenue by 2007. (This is just for the sake of creating a simple example; in reality we'd want an empirical basis for our target.)

In order to achieve $2 million in revenue in 2007, given the small number of addressable handsets, we need a 5 percent sell-through rate. Now we can have a conversation about whether that is achievable, centered on key questions: Have we done it before? Is this a must-have application? Will we have competition? Have any other paid applications achieved this penetration? Will a competitor offer something for less money or free? Is

2007 the right target year? We transformed the conversation from one about financial modeling to marketing and strategy facilitated by our model.

SETTING THE COST OF CAPITAL

The cost of capital is the rate of return an investment should be expected to earn. Whether it is an M&A transaction or upgrading a piece of equipment, the same principles apply. The cost of capital is the weighted average cost of capital (WACC), which reflects the blended cost of equity and debt appropriate for the investment. The cost of debt and equity are weighted based on market value, not book value.

$$\text{WACC} = \text{Cost of Equity} \times (1 - D/TMV) + \text{Cost of Debt}$$
$$\times (1 - T) \times D/TVM$$

Take note of how we define these variables:

Cost of Equity = Risk-Free Rate + Equity Risk Premium.
Equity Risk Premium = Beta × RPF × Risk-Free Rate.
RPF = Risk Premium Factor (currently 1.48).
D = Market Value of All Company Debt.
TMV = Total Market Value of Debt Plus Equity.
Cost of Debt = Incremental Long-Term Borrowing Cost.
T = Marginal Tax Rate.

Beta is a measure of nondiversifiable risk relative to the Standard & Poor's (S&P) 500 reflecting the correlation of returns for a stock with the S&P 500. A beta of 0, means no correlation, a beta of 1.0 means the stock moves the same as the market, while a beta of greater than 1.0 means the stock moves more than the market, so if the market goes down, the stock is expected to fall further, but also gain more on the upside. By definition, beta for the S&P 500 is 1.0. By multiplying the market-wide ERP by beta, we get the company ERP. Beta can be derived as the observed beta for your company. If your company is public, you can look it up or calculate it. It's an important number, but its derivation is beyond the scope of what I am trying to cover. Most data sources, including sites like Yahoo Finance, Google Finance, and brokerage sites provide beta. As a note of caution, sometimes the calculated beta does not make sense. As an extreme example, a thinly traded equity may have a very low beta, sometimes close to zero.

Logically, it does not make sense that this company is riskless. Use good judgment when selecting a beta.

If your company is not public or thinly traded, or for some other reason you suspect the beta you calculate is incorrect, beta also can be derived by looking at peer companies. For example, if you are a private manufacturer of paper products, then base it on the beta for other paper companies. A widely accepted way to do this is to take the beta for each firm and unlever it—that is, approximate beta for a company without debt:

$$\text{Unlevered Beta} = \text{Levered Beta}/(1 + (1 - T) \times (D/E))$$

where D and E are the market value of debt and equity, and T is the marginal tax rate. Calculate the unlevered beta for each firm, take the average, and then relever based on your company's capital structure:

$$\text{Levered Beta} = \text{Unlevered Beta} \times (1 + (1 - T) \times (D/E))$$

The market value of debt is not necessarily the book value. For example, if a company has long-term debt on the books at 10 percent and its current borrowing cost is 5 percent, the market value is higher than face value because of its high yield—if you were to try and buy the debt, you'd have to pay more than face value to make up for the yield. The market value of equity is the value of all the common, preferred, warrants, and options. If the latter are not significant, then it is probably reasonable to ignore them. The cost of debt is the long-term cost of borrowing. The cost of debt is probably not your company's average cost of debt. Your company may have a mix of short- and long-term, secured and unsecured debt instruments as part of its capital structure. While borrowing short term may lower current interest rates, the true measure is your cost of long-term debt.

Ideally, the cost of capital should reflect the WACC for a particular business unit or project. For example, in a highly diversified company like General Electric, it might make sense for each business unit to have its own cost of capital determined as if they are stand-alone businesses. If businesses have different levels of risk, then projects in those businesses should be evaluated using that level of risk. This is fairly straightforward if we assume that the debt capacity is the same for all business units. Simply calculate the cost of equity for the business unit using an appropriate beta as earlier and apply the same debt-to-equity ratio to determine WACC.

Likewise, projects or acquisitions should be evaluated using WACC appropriate for their level of risk. For example, if Utilico, a low-risk power company, decides to build a new power plant, the company WACC is appropriate. But if Utilico decides to start or acquire a new line of business, the WACC needs to be appropriate for the new business.

EXAMPLE: UTILITY ACQUIRING A RISKY ASSET

Let's assume Utilico has a beta of 0.5, can borrow long-term at 6 percent, its debt to market value is 25 percent, and the risk-free rate is 5 percent, then:

Cost of Equity $= 5.0$ percent $(R_f) + 1.48$ (RPF) $\times 0.5$ (Beta) $\times 5.0$ percent

Cost of Equity $= 8.7$ percent

With a marginal tax rate of 40 percent:

$$\text{WACC} = 8.7 \text{ percent} \times 75 \text{ percent (E/TMV)} + 6 \text{ percent}$$
$$\times (1 - 40 \text{ percent (T)}) \times 25 \text{ percent (D/TMV)}$$
$$\text{WACC} = 7.4 \text{ percent}$$

Utilico is considering the acquisition of Riskyco. Riskyco is a promising business with great growth prospects, but Riskyco has very volatile earnings, is not yet very profitable, and has no tangible assets, so it can't borrow. We learn that peer companies to Riskyco have betas around 2.0, giving it a cost of equity of 19.8 percent. Utilico believes that they can bring value to Riskyco by distributing its products to Utilico's customers and greatly increase sales. For the sake of the exercise, let's assume this is true.

What cost of capital should we use to evaluate the acquisition? On the face of it, it does not make sense for low-risk companies like Uitlico to be able to buy high-risk companies like Riskyco and magically create value with by leveraging their lower cost of capital. (If it did, utilities would be buying up the world and being rewarded for it.) You might argue that Riskyco is small, so the risk for Utilico won't change, and the borrowing costs are the borrowing costs, so we should use Utilico's WACC. This would be wrong.

One way to illustrate this fallacy is to play it out at the extreme. If we were to assume that instead of being a small company, Riskyco is large, with a market value equal to Utilico's, then the argument falls apart. Utilico would now be half risky business and its beta would likely rise to the blended average of 1.25. Furthermore, Riskyco would not add any debt capacity, so lenders would view Utilico as more risky, so its cost of debt would rise.

The answer is that Utilico should evaluate Riskyco using a WACC of 19.8 percent—Riskyco's cost of equity. Since it can't support any debt, WACC equals the cost of equity. This is a complicated topic, and this chapter only scratches the surface. If you really want to dive into the subject, I recommend *Cost of Capital: Applications and Examples,* Fourth Edition (Wiley Finance, 2010), by Shannon P. Pratt and Roger J. Grabowski.

SELECTING THE INVESTMENT FORECAST TIME HORIZON

The investment evaluation time horizon is the time period (i.e., number of years) over which you forecast cash flow. Selecting the appropriate time horizon is very important, yet often done incorrectly for a variety of reasons. I recommend two considerations for determining the time horizon:

1. Forecast until growth stabilizes.
2. Forecast to include one complete economic cycle at stable growth.

Before we go into detail about each of these, let's look at some pitfalls and related objections.

Pitfall 1: Forgetting that your forecast model is an expression of as-
    sumptions. The section on establishing your world view describes
    the proper mind-set for developing projections—think of the fore-
    cast as more than numbers but an expression of your point of view
    and uncertainties. The forecast horizon needs to be long enough to
    reflect your worldview or investment thesis.

Pitfall 2: The time horizon is too short. A frequent objection to a longer
    time horizon, especially in emerging sectors, is the high degree of
    future uncertainty and the contention that it needs to be short be-
    cause we can't forecast that far into the future. True enough that
    it's hard to forecast into the next year, let alone the next decade;
    nevertheless, a longer time horizon is the lesser of two evils. Trying
    to cram everything into, say, a five-year forecast not only diminishes
    the effectiveness of your projections but increases the importance of
    your terminal value, effectively camouflaging your uncertainty.

Pitfall 3: Not accounting for economic cycles. The economy is cyclical,
    and this has a large but predictable impact on some businesses.
    Analysts often ignore future downturns because they don't know
    when they will hit. If you are developing a forecast for a cyclical
    business, it is critical to recognize cyclicality.

Pitfall 4: Once size fits all. Companies often have standard templates for evaluating projects and acquisitions. In general, this is a good practice but must be implemented with some flexibility. If a company is evaluating a project or acquisition in a new sector, the standards need to be evaluated to ensure they make sense. The forecast horizon needs to fit to the problem being analyzed.

Pitfall 5: Fear of having an opinion. If you are making a long-term projection, you usually won't have sources of information to guide the out years. You need to state and make assumptions to complete your forecast. Some analysts will either assume the most conservative or no change to develop an out-year forecast. Both of these approaches are dangerous.

Forecast until Growth Stabilizes

Let's revisit our evaluation of the decision to MobAppCo, where we developed a five year projection. We showed rapid growth in an emerging product category but with revenue appearing to come up short, we were on the verge of concluding this project should not be pursued.

Should we abandon the project? Let's dig deeper. In our original projection we stopped at five years but the market was still growing quite rapidly. We also assumed that the number of new handsets sold that would be capable of running our application would top out at 50 percent because that was all the data we had. Our analyst report said 50 percent in three years, and we could not find any source to provide a longer-term projection. This is not an unusual situation. If fact, it is probably the rule rather than the exception. Absent an expert forecast, many analysts will assume either the most conservative stance or status quo. Both of these can lead to poor decision making.

In this situation we only projected growth in the number of addressable handsets sold as long as we had a forecast to back it up. While this is conservative, it is also unreasonable. It is akin to taking a five-year forecast for the U.S. economy and assuming that growth stops in year 5. Ridiculous, right? If the percentage of new handsets sold that are addressable is expected to grow from 6 percent in 2006 to 50 percent in 2008, it is obviously reasonable to assume it will continue growing. In fact, absent some compelling evidence that 50 percent is the upper limit, it is just silly, not conservative. Following this logic could easily cause your business to lose out on a valuable market opportunity.

We need to develop our own set of projections. For example, if we know that the limiting factor on the number of addressable handsets sold is only cost, and we know that costs are expected to fall, as costs for electronics always do, then we should expect that at some point all new handsets will be addressable. Now all we need to decide is when that will happen and bake the assumption into our forecast ... and state it as an important assumption and one rationale for the investment. Rather than placing an artificial limit on our forecast horizon, we extend it from 5 years to 10 years. At the 10-year mark with all new and existing handsets capable of running our application, the market has stabilized.

Another problem with the original projections was the assumption that we would have a 1 percent sell-through rate. Upon further analysis, we conclude that the sell-through rate should exceed 1 percent after a few years. Finally, we revisit pricing. We assumed $2 per month for the first three years and are still confident that this is reasonable, but we expect prices to decline beyond year 3 before stabilizing. In this case, assuming the status quo would have led us to overestimate revenue. Table 7.3 shows the revised revenue projections.

The revenues begin to look much more interesting, rising from $1.1 million in 2008 to $30.7 million in 2015. Adhering to a shorter time horizon or reluctance to formulate our own worldview would have caused us to miss this opportunity. While we are admittedly uncertain regarding revenues in the out years, the forecast allows us to express the financial impact resulting from our key assumptions.

Now that we have our 10-year projection, we will add cost projections. For simplicity, we are assuming that all investment is expensed in the year incurred. Beyond that, we project heavy marketing costs while we are building share, but they drop in 2015 after we stop increasing share. If we take the NPV of this 10-year projection, it is −$6.3 million despite strong earnings in the out years. While we did project the cash flow until the business stabilized in 2015, we still need to determine the value beyond our forecast horizon. The next chapter deals with terminal value.

THE ALL-IMPORTANT TERMINAL VALUE

The terminal value captures value beyond the forecast horizon. That value depends on your assumptions about the future.

The most common approaches are:

- Liquidation value
- Exit multiple
- Perpetuity

Let's start by dispensing with the first two. The only time to use liquidation value is if the project is not a going concern, meaning that you do not expect it to generate cash flow beyond the horizon. Exit multiples are

TABLE 7.3 10-Year Projection

$ Millions	2006	2007	2008	2009	2010	2011	2012	2013	2014	2015
Revenue Forecast										
Existing Addressable Handsets	3.0	8.0	25.9	70.3	134.3	196.5	208.3	218.4	227.6	236.2
Number Handsets Sold in United States	100.0	103.0	106.1	109.3	112.6	115.9	119.4	123.0	126.7	130.5
% Addressable	6%	20%	50%	80%	95%	100%	100%	100%	100%	100%
Total Addressable Sold	6.0	20.6	53.0	87.4	106.9	115.9	119.4	123.0	126.7	130.5
Addressable of Handsets Retired	(1.0)	(2.7)	(8.6)	(23.4)	(44.8)	(104.1)	(109.2)	(113.8)	(118.1)	(122.2)
Ending Addressable Handsets	8.0	25.9	70.3	134.3	196.5	208.3	218.4	227.6	236.2	244.5
Average Addressable Handsets	5.5	17.0	48.1	102.3	165.4	202.4	213.4	223.0	231.9	240.3
Target Market @ 10%	0.55	1.70	4.81	10.23	16.54	20.24	21.34	22.30	23.19	24.03
Sell-through Rate	0.3%	0.5%	1.0%	2.0%	4.0%	6.0%	7.0%	8.0%	9.0%	10.0%
Avg. Customers	0.00	0.01	0.05	0.20	0.66	1.21	1.49	1.78	2.09	2.40
Rev. Customer/Month	2.00	2.00	2.00	1.60	1.28	1.02	1.03	1.04	1.06	1.07
Annual Revenue	0.03	0.20	1.16	3.93	10.16	14.92	18.54	22.37	26.42	30.73

Income Statement

Revenue	0.03	0.20	1.16	3.93	10.16	14.92	18.54	22.37	26.42	30.73
Sales and Marketing	2.50	2.50	2.50	2.75	7.11	10.44	12.97	15.66	18.50	12.29
Product Development	1.00	1.00	1.00	1.00	1.02	1.49	1.85	2.24	2.64	3.07
EBIT	(3.47)	(3.30)	(2.34)	0.18	2.03	2.98	3.71	4.47	5.28	15.37
Tax	(1.39)	(1.32)	(0.94)	0.07	0.81	1.19	1.48	1.79	2.11	6.15
Net Income	(2.08)	(1.98)	(1.41)	0.11	1.22	1.79	2.22	2.68	3.17	9.22

Cash Flow

Capex	(0.60)	(0.60)	(0.60)	(0.60)	(0.60)	(0.60)	(0.60)	(0.60)	(0.60)	(0.60)
Depreciation	0.60	0.60	0.60	0.60	0.60	0.60	0.60	0.60	0.60	0.60
Operating Cash Flow	(2.08)	(1.98)	(1.41)	0.11	1.22	1.79	2.22	2.68	3.17	9.22

quite common. The idea is to assign a value to the business at the end of the horizon equal to what you would realize in a sale. While the concept is sound, the execution is often flawed.

One problem with using exit multiples is that they are frequently determined by using current market multiples, implicitly assuming the market will be the same in the future as it is today. This could cause a large overstatement. For example, continuing with our example of MobAppCo, the mobile application development company, if we were to look at comparables today, they would likely have big growth expectations that should be played out by the end of our forecast horizon. As a result, current market multiples would be large relative to the mature business it will become at the end of the forecast period. Once again, let's look at some pitfalls and related objections.

> **Pitfall 1: Using a too-low exit multiple.** I have heard executives argue to use 5 × earnings before interest, taxes, depreciation, and amortization (EBITDA) as terminal value on the basis that they want to have a 20 percent return on investment (ROI) rather than a market-based value. When we suggest that another way to view terminal value is the value of the business in the final year, they suggest that market value does not matter since they would never sell it. While 5× may be the right multiple, it should be based on market value, not investor preference. This approach can systematically understate value. Understand that this might be a conscious decision on the part of leadership to make valuations more conservative since they believe that forecasts are generally too optimistic to begin with.

> **Pitfall 2: Using today's market multiples.** Since you should be running your forecast until the business stabilizes, today's multiples on growth businesses will always overstate value at the end of your forecast horizon.

> **Pitfall 3: Being overly conservative on terminal value because it accounts for too much of NPV.** The percentage of value accounted for in NPV is entirely a function of the length of your forecast horizon. The longer the forecast horizon, the smaller the percentage. It only goes to illustrate the fallacy of picking a short horizon by reasoning that the future is foggy.

> **Pitfall 4: Not normalizing final-year cash flow.** Examples include final-year cash flow containing nonrecurring expenses, not accounting for equipment near end of life, or calculating at top or bottom of the cycle. Each of these will distort your terminal value.

Now that we have exposed the pitfalls, we can look at the proper way to set the set terminal value. Terminal value is simply the value of cash flows beyond your forecast horizon, usually in perpetuity.

Perpetuity Is a Long Time

The perpetuity value of final-year cash flows can be calculated using the constant growth equation—a perpetuity formula—similar to that used in the RPF Model:

$$\text{Terminal Value (TV)} = \text{OCF}/(\text{WACC} - \text{G})$$

In this equation, OCF is normalized final-year operating cash flow, WACC is the weighted average cost of capital, and G is the long-term growth rate. Because we are using the estimate of final-year cash flow in perpetuity (i.e., forever), it is important that we get the variables right.

While WACC for the terminal value does not change, it is important to recognize and understand the implicit assumptions. WACC assumes that tax rates and capital structure are static in perpetuity. While most practitioners will agree with this assumption, it is important to acknowledge and consider whether it is valid for your company. If you expect capital structure or tax rate to change, then the WACC should change based on projected capital structure. If you expect leverage to decline over time, such as in the case of a leveraged buyout, then WACC should change based on projected capital structure in each forecast year.

Estimating G—Long-Term Growth Rate

Some practitioners, under the guise of being conservative, will calculate the terminal value based on a perpetuity that ignores growth. This is a mistake.

$$\text{G} = \text{Long-Term Real Growth} + \text{Inflation}$$

The long-term growth rate is composed of two components—inflation and real growth—which should be viewed, discussed, and applied separately. Because WACC includes inflation in both the cost of equity and cost of debt, inflation must be accounted for in the terminal value. If the terminal value assumes no growth, it is implicitly assuming that cash flow will shrink in real terms since it does not grow with inflation. Because this is usually not the case, the assumption should then be highlighted in your analysis. Fortunately, as we've seen, the long-term inflation rate is easy to determine since it is a component of WACC derived by subtracting the long-term

TABLE 7.4 Terminal Value Inputs

Inputs		Notes
R_f	5.00%	30-year Treasury yield
RPF	1.48	
Beta	1.4	Company beta
Long-Term Growth Rate (G_R)	2.60%	Assumed to grow at pace with economy
Real Interest Rate	2.00%	Std. RPF Model assumption
Cost of Debt	6.50%	Actual
Marginal Tax Rate	40%	Actual
D/TMV	20%	Actual/forecast
Calculated Values		
Implied Inflation	3.00%	R_f – Real Interest Rate
Equity Risk Premium	7.40%	$R_f \times$ RPF
Company Risk Premium	10.4%	ERP $\times$ Beta
Cost of Equity	15.4%	R_f + Company Risk Premium
WACC	13.1%	
TV Multiple	**13.4**	1 / (WACC – Implied Inflation – G_R)

real interest rate from the risk-free rate. In the terminal value calculation in Table 7.4, the implied long-term inflation rate is 3 percent, based on a 5 percent risk-free rate and 2 percent real interest rate.

Establishing real growth is more subjective, but some general guidelines apply. First, since we are creating a set of projections that extend until the target business reaches a relatively steady state, growth should not exceed that of the overall economy. Since we use 2.6 percent as the long-term growth rate for the economy in determining the cost of equity in the RPF Model, this is a good starting point.

The question is now how fast you expect the business to grow relative to the overall economy. In some businesses, this is a simple decision. For example, in a construction-related business we might know that the long-term trend has been for average growth to equal economic growth, so using 2.6 percent is a reasonable assumption.

What about growth businesses like our emerging mobile application business? This is more difficult to substantiate. High-tech businesses tend to grow rapidly, then plateau or even decline, so negative real growth might be justified. But this approach ignores the option value—the fact that entering a new business creates future options—things that we can't anticipate today that could generate future opportunities arising out of the core business. While the core business might decline, we can make a strong argument that the customer relationships create significant value in that they will enable us to sell next-generation products. This is really no different than putting in future product development costs or capital expenditures for products we cannot anticipate today—funding for that next generation.

An argument can be made for below-average long-term growth on the basis that our target business has exited its prime growth phase, so long-term growth should be below average. The "easy out" is to assume no real growth under the guise of being conservative. While conservative, it may lead to poor decisions. A better approach for estimating growth is to create a set of "future comps." *Comps,* short for comparables, is a term used to describe a set of peer companies used as a comparison, often for the purpose of establishing valuation multiples, beta, margins, growth, or other financial metrics. Future comps are companies that today have characteristics similar to what you expect of your target at the end of the forecast horizon. With the MobAppCo, we might consider a set of today's application software companies as the comparable peer set. If we look back to Chapter 6 on RIGR analysis, Table 6.2 shows RIGR for a selection of software companies and we see that they rank at the 57th percentile in growth and above the S&P 500 average. This provides an argument for assuming that the business will continue to grow with the economy.

Sensitivity analysis can help understand the relative importance of these assumptions. The longer the forecast horizon and the more early-year cash flow, the less your total valuation will change with growth rate assumptions. PV (the value of the business, not NPV) may fall by more than 20 percent when real growth is ratcheted down from 2.6 percent to 0 percent.

In this case it appears that assuming long-term growth is the same as the economy is reasonable. If you are inclined to select a growth rate faster than the economy, it is likely that your forecast horizon is too short. If you choose a low long-term growth, you are being conservative but not necessarily making a better decision.

Normalizing Final-Year Cash Flow

Because final-year cash flow is the basis of the terminal value, it is important to get it right. The next two chapters provide examples illustrating the extremes: a high-growth business based on our MobAppCo example and a low-growth cyclical business based on a building materials manufacturer.

For the high-growth company, the terminal value cash flow is simply the final-year cash flow (i.e., the cash flow after the growth has subsided). For the cyclical business, the final-year cash flow is based on the average through an economic cycle. These will be discussed in the next two chapters.

Calculating Terminal Value Multiples

Using the RPF Model, the terminal value is reduced to a multiple. Table 7.4 shows the inputs of an example terminal value calculation. Internal consistency is important, so the inputs should be the same inputs used to calculate the cost of capital.

The terminal value multiple is then applied to the normalized final year cash flow.

What if management insists on using EBIT or EBITDA multiple for terminal value? Executives may insist on using a terminal value multiple based on EBIT or EBITDA, simply because that is what they are comfortable with. My advice is to pick your battles. If your chairman is accustomed to using an 8× EBIDTA multiple, before considering a disagreement, first determine if the difference is material. To convert your terminal value to an EBITDA multiple, simply calculate your terminal value, then divide by final year or normalized EBITDA. If your final-year cash flow assumes that depreciation equals capital expenditure (as it probably should), then the EBIT multiple is simply:

$$\text{EBIT Multiple} = \text{Cash Flow TV Multiple} \times (1 - \text{Tax Rate})$$

CHAPTER RECAP

Financial models are a tool, not an end. It is important establish a worldview and use the model to translate that view into numbers with forecasts based on key business drivers that lead to standard financial measures and can be useful to help understand the impact of uncertainties. If forecasts are very uncertain, consider reverse-engineering to test reasonableness (i.e., can we achieve the 5 percent sell-through rate necessary to hit our revenue targets?).

The ERP calculated using the RPF Model can be used to calculate cost of capital. The following is a step-by-step guide for calculating WACC:

1. Determine the following variables:
   a. D = Market value of debt
   b. Cost of debt = Incremental borrowing cost
   c. Risk-free rate (R_f) (usually the long bond rate)
   d. E = Market value of equity, including options, warrants, etc. if material
   e. TMV = D + E
   f. T= Marginal tax rate (not average tax rate)

2. Determine beta. If you know your company beta and it is appropriate for your target or project, us it. Otherwise:
   a. Select a group of peer companies.
   b. Determine the levered beta, D/E, and tax rate for the peers.
   c. Levered beta can be determined by looking up from a reliable source or calculated.
   d. Unlever the peer betas using: Unlevered Beta = Levered Beta / (1 + (1 − Tax Rate) × (D / E))
   e. Take an average of the unlevered peer Betas, then relever using your target D/E using the formula: Levered Beta = Unlevered Beta × (1 + (1 − Tax Rate) × (D / E))
3. Determine cost of equity: Cost of Equity = Beta × RPF × R_f
4. WACC = Cost of Equity × (1 − D / TMV) + Cost of Debt × (1 − T) × D/TMV

One size does not fit all—the horizon should fit the project. Forecasts should be extended until growth stabilizes and, if the economic cylce impacts your projections, include at least one full economic cycle. While it is rare to have a reliable forecast for critical assumptions, taking the most conservative view is generally not the best answer. In these cases, you will need to develop a well-reasoned, fact-based opinion that can be opened to debate and discussion.

Terminal value accounts for a large portion of total value, so it should receive considerable thought and attention. While terminal value may be large, its size is dependent on the length of the forecast horizon, so importance of terminal value can always be reduced by lengthening the forecast horizon, but that introduces potential for other errors. The RPF Model is well suited for calculating terminal value:

$$\text{Terminal Value (TV)} = \text{OCF}/(\text{WACC} - \text{G})$$

whrer G is the long-term real growth rate plus inflation, OCF is normalized final-year cash flow, long-term real growth should be relative to assumptions for the overall economy used in the RPF Model (2.6 percent), and inflation is risk-free rate—real interest rate.

CHAPTER 8

Case Study 1

Valuation of a High-Growth Business

This chapter builds on the principles in previous chapters to value a high-growth company with a focus on selecting forecast time horizon and calculating a terminal value.

This chapter discusses simplified valuation building on the example of MobAppCo, the mobile phone application development business from previous chapters. In this example, we are attempting to value MobAppCo as a potential internal start-up. Since it is assumed that the reader either already has a good understanding of financial projections or is only looking for high-level insights, the financial statements used in the next two chapters have been simplified to make it easier to highlight the most important valuation elements. The example includes only a simplified income statement and cash flow. In practice, you would also develop a balance sheet, depreciation schedule, goodwill amortization schedule, and other appropriate financial forecasting elements.

The first step is to develop the cost of capital following the steps outlined in Chapter 7. Table 8.1 shows the cost of capital calculation for this business. The calculation is based on our assumptions for beta, tax rate, debt to market value, cost of debt, and risk-free rate as specified.

We determine beta based on an analysis of companies in businesses similar to MobAppCo. The last part of this chapter discusses other approaches for dealing with uncertainty.

Because this is a start-up business, it is not technically correct to use a corporate weighted average cost of capital (WACC) that includes debt for discounting cash flows. In its early years, if MobAppCo were a stand-alone business, it would not be able to borrow, so the cost of capital would

TABLE 8.1   Cost of Capital for MobAppCo

Inputs		Notes
R_f	5.0%	30-year Treasury yield
RPF	1.48	
Beta	1.4	Company beta
Long-Term Growth Rate (G_R)	2.6%	Assumed to grow at pace with economy
Real Interest Rate	2.0%	Std. RPF Model assumption
Cost of Debt	6.5%	Actual
Marginal Tax Rate	40%	Actual
D/TMV	20%	Actual/forecast
Calculated Values		
Implied Inflation	3.00%	R_f – Real Interest Rate
Equity Risk Premium	7.4%	$R_f \times$ RPF
Company Risk Premium	10.4%	ERP $\times$ Beta
Cost of Equity	15.4%	R_f + Company Risk Premium
WACC	13.1%	

be equal to the cost of equity. However, it would unfairly penalize the valuation to assume that MobAppCo's cost of capital would be the cost of equity for the entire forecast period. Unfortunately, adjusting for this will increase complexity. The examples that follow will illustrate the different approaches and their impact on valuation.

Many practitioners employ elaborate methods to improve the technical precision of their valuations, but these can add a significant level of complexity. One such adjustment is rather than a assuming a constant cost of capital, the cost of capital could be adjusted each year to account for risk and debt capacity. In this case, since the company gains debt capacity as it matures, WACC would be calculated each year using an appropriate capital structure and beta, resulting in a lower WACC in each year. Another adjustment is midyear discounting. Since most spreadsheets default to assume the cash flow occurs at the end of the period, value is understated if cash flow is actually uniformly distributed throughout the year.

I advise caution in employing these approaches. While more precise, these may not appreciably improve your decision-making process, just add to complexity and potential for error. In addition, introducing too many moving parts can create confusion or skepticism. By introducing another set of assumptions for discussion, it might also create a distraction that takes away from discussing critical issues. Being overly precise also can imply a level of accuracy that is not present in reality. Use your best judgment with due consideration for your standard corporate practices and culture.

Table 8.2 shows the full set of projections beginning with the revenue projection developed in Chapters 7, where we forecast revenues out until we expected growth to stabilize. Working down the page, we forecast sales and marketing expenses and product development, followed by earnings before interest and taxes (EBIT), tax, and net income. The next section in the table includes adjustments for cash flow. For simplicity of this example, we assume depreciation equals capital expenditures. In reality, calculating acquisition depreciation and amortization is more complex. The final-year operating expense in 2015 includes reduced sales and marketing expenses, since our assumption is that at this point we begin to milk the business and growth slows to the long-term rate. We assume the expenses included are sufficient to maintain this expected level of growth.

Basing the terminal value on an internally consistent normalized cash flow and growth is critical. It would have been inconsistent to assume that sales and marketing expenses did not decline in the final year but growth did decline. The terminal value multiple is calculated in Table 8.3. Remember, the formula is

$$\text{Terminal Value Multiple} = 1/C - G$$

where

$C = \text{WACC}$
$G = \text{Real growth plus inflation}$

So using the inputs from Table 8.3:

$$\text{Terminal Value Multiple} = 1/(13.1 \text{ percent} - 3 \text{ percent} - 2.6 \text{ percent})$$
$$= 13.4$$

As shown in Table 8.3, this is multiplied by the normalized terminal-year cash flow, resulting in a terminal value of $123.45 million. For comparison purposes, you can divide this value by earnings before interest, taxes, depreciation, and amortization (EBITDA) and EBIT to determine the equivalent EBITDA and EBIT multiples, in this case, 7.7× and 8.0×, respectively. Working through the remainder of Table 8.2, we calculate the nominal cash flows including terminal value and discount them to present at WACC. The resulting value is $39.07 million, and subtracting the initial investment of $10 million yields a net present value (NPV) of $29.07 million; $39.07 million represents the intrinsic value of operations.

TABLE 8.2 Example Valuation: MobAppCo

$ Millions	2006	2007	2008	2009	2010	2011	2012	2013	2014	2015	Normalized
Revenue Forecast											
Existing Addressable Handsets	3.0	8.0	25.9	70.3	134.3	196.5	208.3	218.4	227.6	236.2	
Number Handsets Sold in United States	100.0	103.0	106.1	109.3	112.6	115.9	119.4	123.0	126.7	130.5	
% Addressable	6%	20%	50%	80%	95%	100%	100%	100%	100%	100%	
Total Addressable Sold	6.0	20.6	53.0	87.4	106.9	115.9	119.4	123.0	126.7	130.5	
Addressable of Handsets Retired	(1.0)	(2.7)	(8.6)	(23.4)	(44.8)	(104.1)	(109.2)	(113.8)	(118.1)	(122.2)	
Ending Addressable Handsets	8.0	25.9	70.3	134.3	196.5	208.3	218.4	227.6	236.2	244.5	
Average Addressable Handsets	5.5	17.0	48.1	102.3	165.4	202.4	213.4	223.0	231.9	240.3	
Target Market @ 10%	0.55	1.70	4.81	10.23	16.54	20.24	21.34	22.30	23.19	24.03	
Sell-through Rate	0.3%	0.5%	1.0%	2.0%	4.0%	6.0%	7.0%	8.0%	9.0%	10.0%	
Avg. Customers	0.00	0.01	0.05	0.20	0.66	1.21	1.49	1.78	2.09	2.40	
Rev. Customer/Month	2.00	2.00	2.00	1.60	1.28	1.02	1.03	1.04	1.06	1.07	
Annual Revenue	0.03	0.20	1.16	3.93	10.16	14.92	18.54	22.37	26.42	30.73	

Income Statement

Revenue	0.03	0.20	1.16	3.93	10.16	14.92	18.54	22.37	26.42	30.73
Sales and Marketing	2.50	2.50	2.50	2.75	7.11	10.44	12.97	15.66	18.50	12.29
Product Development	1.00	1.00	1.00	1.00	1.02	1.49	1.85	2.24	2.64	3.07
EBIT	(3.47)	(3.30)	(2.34)	0.18	2.03	2.98	3.71	4.47	5.28	15.37
Tax	(1.39)	(1.32)	(0.94)	0.07	0.81	1.19	1.48	1.79	2.11	6.15
Net Income	(2.08)	(1.98)	(1.41)	0.11	1.22	1.79	2.22	2.68	3.17	9.22

Cash Flow

Capex	(0.60)	(0.60)	(0.60)	(0.60)	(0.60)	(0.60)	(0.60)	(0.60)	(0.60)	(0.60)
Depreciation	0.60	0.60	0.60	0.60	0.60	0.60	0.60	0.60	0.60	0.60
Operating Cash Flow	(2.08)	(1.98)	(1.41)	0.11	1.22	1.79	2.22	2.68	3.17	9.22

Terminal Value Calculations

TV Multiple = 13.4

Terminal Value										123.45
Cash Flow/Terminal Value	(2.08)	(1.98)	(1.41)	0.11	1.22	1.79	2.22	2.68	3.17	132.67

Initial Investment	($10.00)
PV Cash Flows	$39.07
NPV	$29.07

TABLE 8.3   Growth Business Terminal Value Multiple

Inputs		Notes
R_f	5.00%	30-year Treasury yield
RPF	1.48	
Beta	1.4	Company beta
Long-Term Growth Rate (G_R)	2.60%	Assumed to grow at pace with economy
Real Interest Rate	2.00%	Std. RPF Model assumption
Cost of Debt	6.50%	Actual
Marginal Tax Rate	40%	Actual
D/TMV	20%	Actual/forecast
Calculated Values		
Implied Inflation	3.00%	R_f – Real Interest Rate
Equity Risk Premium	7.40%	R_f × RPF
Company Risk Premium	10.4%	ERP × Beta
Cost of Equity	15.4%	R_f + Company Risk Premium
WACC	13.1%	
TV Multiple	**13.4**	1 / (WACC – Implied Inflation – G_R)
EBITDA Multiple	7.7	TV / Final-Year EBITDA
EBIT Multiple	8.0	TV / Final-Year EBIT

As discussed earlier, Table 8.2 calculates the present value using the acquirer's WACC and assumes cash flows occur at the end of each year. A more precise but complicated approach is to calculate an appropriate WACC for each year of the forecast and then discount that year's cash flow based on the cumulative discount factor. The second adjustment is for midyear discounting, where we approximate a cash flow that occurs uniformly throughout each year. The midyear adjustment is the easier of the two. Rather than adjust the discounted cash flow in each year, a good approximation is to simply adjust the final present value by half the WACC. This increases the present value (PV) by half a year, which is the same as having cash flows in midyear. Table 8.4 shows how this is applied.

Another approach to mid-year discounting which is technically more accurate is to multiply by $(1 + \text{WACC})^{0.5} - 1$, rather than WACC / 2. Following the this approach the adjustment factor would be $2,48 million rather than the $2.55 million in Table 8.4.[1] Given that this adjustment is just an approximation that assumes cash flows are distributed evenly through each year, the difference is immaterial, so either approach is reasonable. I err on the side of using an approach that I find easier to explain conceptually.

TABLE 8.4 Adjustment for Midyear
Discounting

PV Cash Flows	$39.07
Adjustment Factor	0.065
Midyear Adjustment	$2.55
PV	$41.62
Initial Investment	($10.00)
NPV	$31.62

Adjusting for changes in WACC over the forecast horizon is a bit more complicated. At the extreme you might need to calculate the debt capacity in each year to estimate the appropriate debt-to-capital ratio for calculating WACC, estimate cost of debt, and even adjust the beta each year to account for the changing capital structure. In the example in Table 8.5, to keep it relatively simple, we assume the cost of capital makes a single step change from the cost of equity to corporate WACC including debt in 2011. This seems appropriate since in that year the company begins generating enough cash to support a 20 percent debt load. In this example, WACC and cost of equity come from Table 8.1.

Table 8.5 begins by showing the cost of capital in each year in the line labeled "Annual WACC." The next line is the cash flow from Table 8.2, followed by the discount factor. The discount factor is calculated by taking the one plus current year cost of capital and multiplying by the discount factor from the prior year. In each year the cash flow is divided by the discount factor to derive the present value of the cash flow from each year. Summing up the discounted cash flows results in the total PV. Note that if the cost of capital is the same in each year, this will yield the same result as a present value calculation using the built-in functions in Excel. The PV is then adjusted for the midyear discounting and the NPV is calculated by subtracting the initial investment.

You can see that this approach lowers the unadjusted present value from $39.07 to $35.08—about 10 percent—due to the much higher cost of capital in the early years. As a point of reference, using the cost of equity rather than WACC in all years and in calculation of the terminal value would lower the unadjusted present value by 24 percent. While more complicated, adjusting the cost of capital does make a material difference.

While it is easy to include all these adjustments into a spreadsheet, I caution that adding complexity introduces additional points for failure and makes it much more difficult for readers to follow.

TABLE 8.5 Adjusted Annual Cost of Capital to Reflect Debt Capacity

$ Millions	2006	2007	2008	2009	2010	2011	2012	2013	2014	2015
Annual WACC	15.4%	15.4%	15.4%	15.4%	15.4%	13.1%	13.1%	13.1%	13.1%	13.1%
Cash Flow/Terminal Value	(2.08)	(1.98)	(1.41)	0.11	1.22	1.79	2.22	2.68	3.17	132.67
Discount Factor	1.15	1.33	1.54	1.77	2.04	2.31	2.61	2.95	3.34	3.78
Annual PV Cash Flow	(1.80)	(1.49)	(0.92)	0.06	0.60	0.78	0.85	0.91	0.95	35.14
Total PV Cash Flow	35.08									
Midyear Adjustment	$2.29									
PV	$37.37									
Initial Investment	($10.00)									
NPV	$27.37									

CALCULATING ENTERPRISE VALUE AND STOCK PRICE

What if, instead of evaluating an acquisition or project, we were valuing a publicly traded company? The process is the same. Begin by calculating the PV of the cash flows, then rather than subtracting the initial investment to determine NPV, the PV is adjusted to account for debt, cash and investment. Let's assume our projections in Table 8.3 were for a public company. This company has no debt and $10 million in cash plus an equity investment in another company that is worth $3 million and 500,000 shares outstanding:

$$\text{Value of Equity} = \text{PV of Cash Flow} - \text{Debt} + \text{Cash} + \text{Equity Investments}$$
$$= \$39.07M - \$0 + \$10M + \$3M$$
$$= \$52.07M$$

The PV of cash flow is also the value of operations. Another way of looking at this is that the value of equity is the value of the operations plus any investments that were not in the cash flow, less debt. Since cash and equity investments were not in the cash flow, they count toward the total value. If the company had debt, that would count against the valuation. Now to calculate the intrinsic share price we simply divide enterprise value by the number of shares, so the intrinsic share price is $104.14 ($52.07/ 0.5M shares).

SCENARIO ANALYSIS

This forecast illustrates only one possible outcome. Given the uncertainty in developing forecasts for a start-up (or otherwise), a better approach for dealing with risk is to develop scenarios to represent a range of outcomes. Many analysts develop worst, base, and upside cases. The effectiveness of this approach will depend on your audience. Some executives will always throw out the upside case as unrealistically optimistic or even anchor on the worst case. Others will look at a conservative base case that has a good return but small absolute size and ask whether it is worth the effort, since the result is too small to "move the needle."

None of the outcomes from this type thinking are appealing. Either growth halts because no projects or deals proceed, analysts get overly optimistic by making the worst case less bad and the base case too optimistic, or the bias shifts to favor big deals and big projects that can move the needle. Each of these carries significant downside.

One common approach to dealing with this type of risk is to assign probabilistic weights to each possible outcome. For example, the worst case may be a 20 percent probability, base 70 percent, and upside 10 percent. The expected value can be calculated based on the NPV of each scenario multiplied by its assigned probability. Even though this introduces additional complexity, it also fosters an interesting series of conversations.

Turning our attention back to MobAppCo, if the potential market is sufficiently large, the upside case may have an NPV many times greater than the base case. For example, let's say the upside NPV is $500 million, compared to about $30 million for the base case. While no sane analyst would present the $500 million as a base case, by presenting it as the upside with a low probability, it could ignite the discussion regarding upside potential for the business.

CHAPTER RECAP

The key points in this chapter regard the selection of time horizon and calculation of terminal value. When valuing a high-growth business, extend the forecast horizon until growth stabilizes. Typically, this means that top-line growth is the same or lower than the overall economy and new investment is at a maintenance level. Terminal value should be based on an internally consistent normalized cash flow and growth rate. Long-term real growth in the terminal value can be approximated by identifying mature comparable companies today that are similar to our target in the final years of our forecast horizon and calculating their RIGR. When the range of potential outcomes is large, consider developing several scenarios to illustrate the impact, both positive and negative, on valuation.

CHAPTER 9

Case Study 2
Valuation of a Cyclical Business

This chapter applies the principles in the previous chapters to a valuing a cyclical business. The focus is on forecasting a cycle and establishing normalized cash flow.

Cyclical businesses are actually a bit more complicated to value from a technical standpoint than growth businesses. This is not to say that growth businesses are easy to value; they are not. Forecasting growth businesses is more difficult since assumptions regarding market development, product, and competition are much more uncertain. Cyclical businesses are more complicated in that they require understanding and adjusting for the business cycle in the forecast horizon and terminal value. But their identification as cyclical by virtue of their having been around for many economic cycles usually means that ample industry data is available.

This chapter will walk through a valuation of a commodity construction materials manufacturer, BlockCo, by another company in the same industry. Since it is assumed that the reader is already competent in developing financial projections, the financial statements used in this example have been simplified in order to make it easier to highlight the most important valuation elements. Our target is a public company with 10.1 million shares outstanding, trading at about $14 per share with $20 million in debt and $5 million cash. It has no other investments.

Enterprise value or total market value is the value of equity plus debt less cash. It represents the cost to acquire a company at the current stock price and including the debt obligations assumed. Since you would also get to keep the cash, it is subtracted. Think of it this way: If you pay $1 million to buy all the stock of a company that has $99 million in debt, you've bought that $99 million debt, and future cash flow will go toward debt service. However, if that company also had $99 million in cash, that could go toward repaying the debt.

Because we already know share price and shares for our target company, we can calculate the enterprise value as $14 × 10.1 million + $20 million − $5 million = $156.4 million. We can calculate the implied value of operations using the formula for value of equity:

Value of Equity = Value of Operations + Cash + Investments − Debt

$141.4M = Value of Operations + $5M + $0 − $20M

Value of Operations = $156.4M

Since there are no other investments, the value of operations is equal to the enterprise value. We know that in order for us to be in a position to make an attractive offer to the shareholder of our target, the operations need to be worth at least $156.4 million. Now we will develop our forecast of operations in order to determine how much we can afford to pay. First, we will develop the cost of capital. Table 9.1 shows the cost of capital calculation for this business.

Even though the target company is currently carrying only about 12 percent debt, we base weighted average cost of capital (WACC) on the acquiring company capital structure and cost of debt. In this case, since the target is in the same industry, the main characteristics of the business are the same as the acquirer, so beta, capital structure, cost of debt, and tax rate can be assumed to be the same for both companies. This assumes that

TABLE 9.1 Cost of Capital for a Cyclical Business

Inputs		Notes
R_f	5.00%	30-year Treasury yield
RPF	1.48	
Beta	1.0	Company beta
Cost of Debt	6.50%	Actual
Marginal Tax Rate	40%	Actual
D/TMV	20%	Actual/forecast
Calculated Values		
Equity Risk Premium	7.40%	R_f × RPF
Company Risk Premium	7.4%	ERP × Beta
Cost of Equity	12.4%	R_f + Company Risk Premium
WACC	10.7%	

we intend to maintain the same capital structure postacquisition and over the long term.

Table 9.2 shows the full set of projections. In order to separate real volume from price, we begin with the initial revenue projections for 2006, then adjust them using a price index in following years by assuming that indexed price is 100 in the base year, so volume equals 2006 revenue. This way, we can forecast volume to match our construction forecasts and adjust price based on inflation with an allowance for cyclical declines. We assume that over the long term, price matches average inflation. It is important to keep the model internally consistent, so the assumed inflation rate should be consistent with our assumptions for risk-free rate and real interest rates.

Because we are developing this forecast in 2005, we can simplify our valuation by blissfully ignoring the cataclysmic declines to come, but this does not mean we ignore recessions. I cannot recall ever seeing an economic forecast that anticipates a recession, so we cannot rely on industry forecasts. We need to develop our own view. Even though we don't know exactly when the economy will fall into recession, our projections are improved by making reasonable assumptions that capture the impact of future cyclicality on value of this business. Since this is a mature industry with a body of historical data, we can analyze past data to help inform our view of the future. Ideally, we would like to figure out how often construction recessions hit, along with the impacts on price and volume. Looking at the historical value of put-in-place construction from the U.S. Bureau of the Census, we can evaluate historical patterns.

Figure 9.1 shows the value of construction from 1964 to 2009 in constant dollars. Since we are assuming the decision is taking place in 2005 to 2006, data only through 2005 is valid for analysis. For those interested, I've presented data through 2009 to show the impact of the recession. This data series was selected since revenue for the business we are evaluating correlates to national construction. Data prior to 1964 was not available. If it were, we would need to determine if it were applicable.

Figure 9.1 shows clear trends of cyclicality and real growth. Table 9.3 breaks this down by looking at trough-to-trough trends to establish the average length of each downturn along with the depth of decline. Troughs rather than peaks were chosen because we have more troughs than peaks, thus more data points in the data set, and they are more easily identifiable than the peaks, which were sometimes less sharp.

We can see that the average cycle length was about seven years and the decline about 12 percent. We assume a seven-year cycle with four up years and three down years, with a real decline in revenues of 12 percent from each peak.

TABLE 8.2 Example Valuation: Cyclical Business

$ Millions	2006	2007	2008	2009	2010	2011	2012	2013	2014	Normalized
Income Statement										
Volume	161.0	177.1	186.0	182.2	180.4	175.0	183.8	192.9	202.6	
Nominal Price Index	100%	103%	106%	109%	109%	108%	114%	117%	121%	
Nominal Revenue	161.0	182.4	197.3	199.1	197.1	189.3	208.7	225.7	244.1	
Real Revenue (Constant 2014 $)	203.9	224.3	235.6	230.9	221.9	206.9	221.4	232.5	244.1	
Real Rev. % Chg		10%	5%	−2%	−4%	−7%	7%	5%		5%
Cost of Goods	101.8	114.0	122.4	123.5	122.4	117.9	129.0	138.7	149.2	
SG&A	24.1	24.8	25.5	26.3	27.1	27.9	28.7	29.6	30.5	
EBITDA	35.2	43.7	49.3	49.3	47.7	43.5	51.0	57.5	64.5	
Depreciation	16.1	18.2	19.7	19.9	19.9	19.9	20.9	22.6	24.4	
EBIT	19.1	25.4	29.6	29.4	27.8	23.6	30.2	34.9	40.1	
PBT	19.1	25.4	29.6	29.4	27.8	23.6	30.2	34.9	40.1	
Net Income	11.4	15.3	17.8	17.7	16.7	14.2	18.1	20.9	24.1	

$ Millions	2006	2007	2008	2009	2010	2011	2012	2013	2014	Normalized
Cash Flow										
Net Income	11.4	15.3	17.8	17.7	16.7	14.2	18.1	20.9	24.1	
Depreciation	16.1	18.2	19.7	19.9	19.9	19.9	20.9	22.6	24.4	
Less: Capex	17.7	20.1	21.7	21.9	21.9	21.9	23.0	24.8	26.9	
Chg. Working Capital	-	-	-	-	-	-	-	-	-	
Operating Cash Flow	9.84	13.43	15.78	15.67	14.68	12.18	16.01	18.69	21.62	21.62
Terminal Value Calculations										
Implied Inflation:	3.00%									
Price Index 2014 Dollars	78.94	81.31	83.75	86.26	88.85	91.51	94.26	97.09	100.00	
Cash Flow 2014 Dollars	12.46	16.52	18.84	18.16	16.53	13.30	16.98	19.25	21.62	
Terminal Value									329.43	17.79
	TV Multiple =		18.52							
Cash Flow/Terminal Value	9.84	13.43	15.78	15.67	14.68	12.18	16.01	18.69	351.05	
Value of Operations (PV Cash Flows)	$214.12									

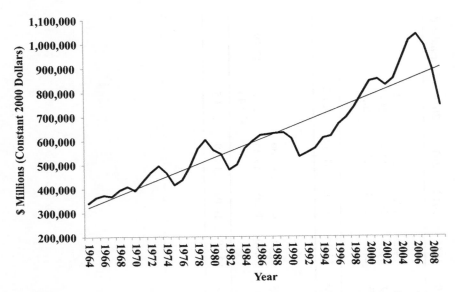

FIGURE 9.1 Value of U.S. Construction Put in Place (Constant 2000 Dollars)
Sources: U.S. Bureau of the Census ("Annual Value of Construction Put in Place
2002–2009," December 8, 2010, www.census.gov/const/www/sitemap.html;
"Annual Value of Construction Put in Place in the United States Current Dollars
1964–2002," December 8, 2010, www.census.gov/pub/); U.S. Budget GDP
Deflators ("Budget of the United States Government: Historical Tables Fiscal Year
2009," Government Printing Office, December 8, 2010, www.gpoaccess.gov/
usbudget/fy09/hist.html), author's analysis (statistics for the two available periods,
1964 to 2002 and 2002 to 2009, were combined the adjusted to constant 2000
dollars using the published GDP deflator).

TABLE 9.3 Analysis of Construction Trends

Trough Year	Years from Peak	Trough Value Constant 2000 $M	Peak Value Constant 2000 $M	Real Decline
1967		368,488		
1970	4	391,750	409,458	−4.3%
1975	5	466,396	495,588	−16.1%
1982	7	479,129	603,969	−20.7%
1991	9	532,421	633,208	−15.9%
2002	11	828,325	852,553	−2.8%
Average	7.2			−12.0%

Sources: U.S. Bureau of the Census, U.S. Budget GDP Deflators, author's analysis.

TABLE 9.4 Long-Term Real Growth Rate (Construction Put in Place)

Time Period	Real Growth Rate	Comment
1964 to 2006	2.7%	Full data set but measures trough to peak
1967 to 2002	2.3%	Longest trough-to-trough period
1966 to 2006	2.6%	Longest peak-to-peak period
1973 to 2006	2.3%	Long peak to peak
1975 to 2002	2.6%	Long trough to trough
1979 to 2006	2.0%	Peak to peak

Sources: U.S. Bureau of the Census, U.S. Budget GDP Deflators, author's analysis.

This is a very simple and straightforward analysis, but has a number of potential pitfalls. First, we selected the time period solely based on available data. While this may be the best approach, I strongly encourage thinking about whether you can get additional data and whether it makes sense to use the data you have. In this case, 1964 to 2006 seems reasonable. Second, we are assuming that this historical period is a reasonable proxy for the future. Since our data set represents a long postwar period that contains several economic shocks, it would seem to be a reasonable proxy. Third, we want to have confidence that revenues for our target actually correlate to the data set. For example, a company that does all its business in one city or region may not correlate to national trends. My point: don't just grab data—think about whether it makes sense.

This data set also provides us another piece of useful information: the historical long-term growth rate. In order to estimate the long-term growth, we looked at growth over several historical periods, as shown in Table 9.4.

The ranges all produce results in a tight range, giving us comfort in the reasonableness of the assumptions. In order to pick our long-term growth rate, we first throw out the 1964 to 2006 period, since it measures from the bottom of one cycle to the top of another, thus exaggerating growth. Looking at the remaining ranges, 2.3 percent is the median and also reflects the cycles that most closely match the trend line. Since a strong case could be used for any of these, we will also perform a sensitivity analysis using both ends of the range.

The projections incorporate a number of features aimed at producing a good basis for valuation. Revenue is composed of volume, based on the projected revenue in the base year, and a price index starting at 100 percent. This enables us to vary volume and price independently. Price increases during periods of growth, then falls during declines. The purpose of the line for real revenues is for calibrating the severity of our recession expectations. Since our historical construction data showed an average real decline of about 10 percent in spending (revenue) during a recession, we have included a three-year downturn with a total decline of about 12 percent real.

Since we are originating these projections in the 2005 to 2006 period and do not see an imminent recession, we forecast a few years of market growth along with strong operating improvements (including above-average volume increases) and a downturn beginning in 2009. Again, the most important observation is that despite the fact that economists are not calling for an imminent recession, we are stilling baking one into our forecasts. Consistent with our historical averages, the downturn lasts three years, followed by four years of growth. We then use the final trough-to-peak period to develop an average operating cash flow for use in our terminal value.

Let's review the remainder of the operating projections in Table 9.2. After revenue, we have fixed and variable costs, depreciation, and taxes. Once again, the purpose of this example is not to illustrate the best way to develop a complete financial forecast, so we'll skip the details of how we derived those assumptions.

Next, beginning with net income, we project cash flow. Note that for simplicity of illustration, we assume no change in working capital. The next section shows the cash flows for terminal value calculation. Our goal is to calculate a normalized cash flow to use in the terminal value calculation. We begin with a price index based on our 3 percent implied inflation rate. This is used to develop a price index of 2014 dollars used to normalize the operating cash flow in each year, so we can calculate and cash flow for the final four years in 2014 dollars. This gives us a normalized cash flow that we can use as the basis for the terminal value calculation. For simplicity, we are assuming that working capital does not change and capital expenditures will equal depreciation in perpetuity.

We use the final four years since this will give us the average cash flow through the cycle and it also reflects the period after our operating improvements kicked in. This is important—we modeled our operating improvements, then extended the forecast time period long enough to give us a postimprovement normalized cash flow. Also note that the final-year cash flow is 22 percent higher than the normalized cash flow of $17.79 million. Again, the intent is to give us average cash flow through the cycle. Implicit in the use of the average is the assumption that we will begin another downturn in 2015 extending through 2018. If we were to extend our forecast through that downturn, and back out real growth, we should still have normalized cash flow of $17.79 million in 2014 dollars. Also note that if we based our terminal value on final-year cash flow alone, we would have overstated our terminal value by 22 percent.

TABLE 9.5 Cyclical Business Terminal Value Multiple

Inputs		Notes
R_f	5.00%	30-year Treasury yield
RPF	1.48	
Beta	1.0	Company beta
Long-Term Growth Rate	**2.30%**	Assumed to grow at pace with economy
Real Interest Rate	2.00%	Std. RPF Model assumption
Cost of Debt	6.50%	Actual
Marginal Tax Rate	40%	Actual
D/TMV	20%	Actual/forecast
Calculated Values		
Implied Inflation	3.00%	R_f − Real Interest Rate
Equity Risk Premium	7.40%	$R_f \times$ RPF
Company Risk Premium	7.4%	ERP × Beta
Cost of Equity	12.4%	R_f + Company Risk Premium
WACC	10.7%	
TV Multiple	**18.5**	1/(WACC − Implied Inflation − G_R)
EBITDA Multiple	5.1	
EBIT Multiple	8.2	

Next up is the calculation of terminal value. Table 9.5 show the inputs and results of the terminal value multiple. Remember, the formula is:

$$\text{Terminal value multiple} = 1/C - G$$

where C = WACC and G = real growth plus inflation. Using the inputs from Table 9.5:

$$\text{Terminal Value Multiple} = 1/(10.7 \text{ percent} - 3 \text{ percent} - 2.3 \text{ percent})$$
$$= 18.1$$

As shown in Table 9.2, this is multiplied by the normalized terminal-year cash flow, resulting in a terminal value of $329.43. For reference, you can divide this value by EBITDA and EBIT to determine the equivalent EBITDA and EBIT multiples; in this case, 5.1× and 8.2×, respectively. Note that these multiples were calculated based on final-year EBITDA and EBIT, so it is not a direct comparison to the TV multiple. The figures could obviously be calculated based on average or normalized EBITDA and EBIT. Working through the remainder of Table 9.2, we calculate the nominal cash flows,

TABLE 9.6 Calculating Intrinsic Share Price

	Millions
Value of Operations	$214.12
+ Cash	3.00
+ Investments	—
− Debt	(20.00)
Value of Equity	197.12
Number of Shares	10.1
Intrinsic Share Price	**$19.52**

including terminal value, and discount them to present at the WACC. The resulting value is $214.12 million.

As a final step in our valuation, we perform a sensitivity analysis on our long-term growth rate and find that increasing the growth rate to 2.6 percent increases our value of operations by $7 million, and lowering the long-term growth rate to 2 percent at the bottom of our range lowers the value of operations by $6.5 million.

Now we need to figure out how much we can pay for the business. First, we calculated the value of equity using the formula, Value of Equity = Value of Operations + Cash + Investments − Debt, then divide by number of shares outstanding, as shown in Table 9.6.

The result shows that based on our projections, the intrinsic value of the shares is $19.52, compared to the market price we quoted earlier of $14, so we can pay a premium of up to 34 percent on the market price and the deal would still be projected to create value. Of course, if all the synergies accrue to the seller, we should probably pass on the deal.

CHAPTER RECAP

The most important differentiator in valuing a cyclical business is to incorporate anticipated cyclicality—even if it is not generally forecast—and extend the growth until all operating improvements are recognized, then far enough to calculate a normalized cash flow that is representative of performance through a business cycle.

CHAPTER 10

Using the RPF Model to Translate Punditry

The varied voices of columnists, writers and sources in financial media are often confusing. This chapter summarizes a selection of recent articles from the financial press and analyzes them through the lens of the Risk Premium Factor (RPF) Model.

The Babel Fish was a fictional animal from Douglas Adams's *Hitchhikers Guide to the Galaxy* that performed translation between alien species. When you consider some of the statements you hear and read related to stock market value, which sometimes seem to be in a different language, investors might long for a similar translator. The varied voices of columnists, writers, and sources in financial media are often confusing. I believe this has many causes. While they are occasionally misguided, others simply focus on the wrong issues or oversimplify; some really get it and explain it well. This chapter summarizes a selection of recent articles from the financial press and then analyzes them through the lens of the RPF Model.

Note that many articles are written to present, not necessarily analyze, the point of views expressed by the subjects quoted in the articles. As such, the selections in this chapter are not meant to suggest that the authors erred in their analysis, but to focus on the themes expressed by the subjects, explain how their comments can be viewed through the lens of the RPF Model, and how readers can better understand how they relate to movement in the market.

READ CAREFULLY, THEN ANALYZE

A *New York Times* article by Jeff Sommer, "Head for the Hills? No Way He Says," on July 17, 2010, recounted a conversation with the author of *Stocks for the Long Run* (McGraw-Hill, 1998) and Wharton professor Jeremy Siegel, where Siegel made the case for confidence in the market: "... when stocks are cheaper than average, as measured by the price-to-earnings ratio, positive returns became more probable in subsequent years."

He went on to say that the price-to-earnings (P/E) ratio was at 13 based on consensus earnings, which was below the long-term average. This is basically a mean reversion argument that stocks have an average P/E and will over time revert to that mean. This implies that P/E should actually be a constant and that any deviation is a pricing error. As we've discussed throughout the book, the mean P/E has little meaning without being put in context relative to interest rates. Based on the RPF Model, the only way there could be a valid mean P/E is if there were also a valid mean interest rate, which in turn implies a valid average inflation. If for a moment you believe that is likely, then revisit Figure 2.1, which shows the yield on the 10-year Treasury since 1960. It shows no evidence of an interest rate cycle.

It says that based on projected earnings stocks are cheap based on a P/E ratio of 13, which is below the historical average. The analysis is based on projected earnings not today's earnings. While this is usually a reasonable approach, it must be recognized since analysts will use a variety of earnings measures. If we apply the RPF Model and assume an interest rate of 4 percent, then the implied P/E ratio is 18.79. Assuming we believe consensus earnings are accurate and interest rates will hold, then the market is even more undervalued than indicated by Siegel.

WHAT HAVE I GOT TO LOSE?

Two weeks earlier, on July 3, 2010, Sommer reported on one market strategist that had a very different view in "A Market Forecast that Says 'Take Cover,'" which undoubtedly prompted the later article. Robert Prechter believed that we were headed into the biggest market decline of the past 300 years. His analysis is based on the Elliot Wave Theory, originated by Ralph Nelson Elliot in the 1930s. Prechter achieved significant notoriety for using the theory to predict the bull market, beginning in 1978, and the 1987 crash. According his web site, www.elliotwave.com:

> The Elliott Wave Principle is a detailed description of how groups of people behave. It reveals that mass psychology swings from pessimism to optimism and back in a natural sequence, creating specific and measurable patterns.
>
> One of the easiest places to see the Elliott Wave Principle at work is in the financial markets, where changing investor psychology is recorded in the form of price movements. If you can identify repeating patterns in prices, and figure out where we are in those repeating patterns today, you can predict where we are going.[1]

The article quoted Prechter as saying:

> *"I'm saying: 'Winter is coming. Buy a coat,'" he said. "Other people are advising people to stay naked. If I'm wrong, you're not hurt. If they're wrong, you're dead. It's pretty benign advice to opt for safety for a while."*[2]

The article goes on to relay Prechter's prediction that the Dow will drop to about 1,000 from about 9,700 when the article was published. He suggested that this would happen over the next five or six years and that investors should completely exit the market and move their assets to cash and Treasury bills. It bears repeating that he is suggesting that the market will fall by more than 90 percent to 1,000, not fall by 1,000 points. Where do we begin? First and most obvious, the Elliot Wave Theory implies that the market is driven solely by trading psychology. As we've seen, it is earnings and interest rates that drive the market. If a theory like this were to have theoretical validity, it would be that the trading patterns in the stock market convey information relating to investor expectations.

One additional statement that can't go unchallenged is Prechter's saying, "If I'm wrong, you're not hurt." Really? If you pull all of your money out of the market and it goes up significantly, not only are you hurt, you are hurt badly. Imagine, if you had $1 million in the market on September 30, 2008. The Standard & Poor's (S&P) 500 was up 5 percent to 1,166 that day after having fallen almost 9 percent the previous day, but was still down 10 percent for the month. You, like everyone else, are nervous, but you decide to hold tight. Fast forward: The S&P 500 falls 17 percent further in October, almost 8 percent in November, then appears to stabilize before falling to 676 on March 9, 2009. Your $1 million is now just $580,000—losing 42 percent on paper. Everyone is in a panic and the pressure to sell is overwhelming. You decide to move 50 percent into cash—what's to lose? By the end of November 2009, the market staged a tremendous comeback with the S&P 500 Index closing at 1,095 on November 30. If you had stayed in the market, your $580,000 would have recovered to $948,000, but instead your 50 percent cash portfolio recovers to only $748,000, locking in a 25 percent loss. At least you didn't lock in a 50 percent loss. Being overly risk averse has a huge opportunity cost.

What if Prechter is right? In order for the Dow to fall to 1,000, unless interest rates rise dramatically, earnings would have to fall about 90 percent. If earnings fell 90 percent, you might have a large fraction of the S&P 500 companies in bankruptcy, massive unemployment, and massive defaults, which might include state and local governments, along with sovereign defaults. At this point, do you even trust the dollar? You might not even be able to hedge this downside because of counterparty risk, since if you are short the S&P 500 the firm on the other end of the trade might default. What's your strategy? The only thing that I can think of is buying a farm, and then at least you can grow your own food.

BEWARE OF OVERSIMPLIFICATION

In a column for the *New York Times* on November 28, 2009, "A Rally that Needs More 'E,'" Paul J. Lim quoted several sources to suggest that the recent gains in the market were due to P/E expansion, and that is likely to have run its course: "On average, the market's P/E tends to peak a little more than a year into a bull market, according to analysis by Ned Davis Research, an investment consulting firm in Venice, Fla."[3]

The idea is that P/E ratios fall as the market falls into recession and grows as it is recovering. From an RPF Model perspective this makes perfect sense. As the market begins to enter a recession, trailing earnings are higher than forecast, and even the forecasts may be overstated. Because the E in P/E is higher than investors expect in the future, stock prices (P) drop, so the P/E ratios drops. As the market recovers, stock prices increase in anticipation of growing earnings, so the P/E ratio increases as P increases faster than the trailing E. Assuming interest rates are steady, this makes sense. Unfortunately, the quote from the analyst above is a bit misleading, since it focuses on P/E expansion relative to the timing of a bull market, rather than the underlying drivers. The timing of the expansion is driven by the pace of economic recovery, which drives earnings. The P/E expands early because the market anticipates earnings growth, then contracts when earnings expectations are realized. You will find that a great deal of analysis refers to the market rather than the underlying drivers. While sometimes it is may be less complicated to explain this way rather than in terms of the underlying economic cycle, it causes confusion by implying that the stock market operates somewhat independently of the economy and corporate performance, which might lead some readers to believe that the market is unpredictable and beyond understanding. As an investor, you need to look behind the façade and understand the factors that drive the market.

The article then continues with a discussion of earnings projections that supports my lead/lag explanation of the P/E contraction and expansion. It quotes Sam Stovall, the chief investment strategist at S&P, who had analyzed bull markets going back to 1942. He found that the average P/E grew by 29 percent during the first year of a bull market, then fell by 6 percent in the second year:

> *In many cases, that's because corporate profits expand so fast that their growth outpaces rising share prices. In other words, as the "E" in the P/E ratio grows faster than the "P," the multiple contracts even as stocks gain ground.*[4]

Of course, P/E declines when P grows slower than E—that's just math. It can't happen any other way. But saying "corporate profits expand so fast that their growth outpaces rising share prices" implies that that market is slow to respond, rather than what actually happens—P increased because the market anticipated the increase in E. While this is likely just an attempt to simplify the story, reading it literally can be confusing. It is important to read into these stories to understand what the author or expert is trying to convey. This becomes clear near the end of the article, where he makes the point that the market needs more E—that you should watch earnings. And, in fact, the article finishes by discussing several prominent analysts' expectations for a significant increase in earnings, which would lead to an increase in stock prices. The key point: analysts expected earnings to rise in 2010, which would drive the market higher—they did and it did.

CONFUSING HEADLINES AND MISGUIDED BLAME

On August 30, 2010, Ben Levisohn wrote "The Decline of the P/E Ratio" for the *Wall Street Journal*. The article starts with the observation that P/E ratios have declined during the past year and are also shrinking in importance as a gauge of fair value, and then discusses the real issue: economic uncertainty. The contention that investors are concerned about earnings is supported with some very interesting observations: "The sustainability of earnings is in doubt," said Howard Silverblatt, an index analyst at S&P in New York. "Estimates are still optimistic."

The article continues to say that the range in analysts' forecast is unusually large, which indicates uncertainty, quoting Jeremy Siegel, professor of finance at the University of Pennsylvania's Wharton School: "The more uncertainty there is, the lower the P/E will be."[5]

The problem outlined is that some analysts believe that earnings are unsustainable and forecasts are too high, while others are more optimistic. The result is a wider-than-usual range of earnings forecasts. This is very interesting from an RPF Model perspective. At the end of August 2010, the RPF model had the S&P undervalued by about 30 percent at its then-current level of 1,049. As you recall, the model is $P = E/(C - G)$. While some might attribute the discrepancy to risk premiums, in that a higher C would lower P, these quotes indicate that investors were fundamentally concerned about whether E was sustainable. The model shows it's not a P/E problem but an E problem.

On September 4, 2010, Levisohn followed up with, "Is It Time to Scrap the Fusty Old P/E Ratio?" Despite the headline, he suggests that the reason valuations seem low relative to the P/E ratio is that investors don't trust earnings. As we've discussed earlier and seen in practice, sometimes when the model predicts a level for the S&P 500 well above actual, the cause is earnings expectations. As an investor, that is exactly where your attention should be focused!

The article goes on to discuss how P/E ratios are often calculated based on projected earnings, and many investors believe these projections are too high and suggests using cash flow rather than earnings for valuation (much like we did in Chapters 8 and 9) and to evaluate enterprise value to free cash flow ratios, which are at a 10-year low:

> The enterprise-value-to-free-cash-flow ratio for the S&P 500 is currently 20, a 10-year low.
>
> Savita Subramanian, head of quantitative strategy at Bank of America Merrill Lynch in New York, says a strategy of buying the 50 cheapest S&P 500 stocks based on the enterprise-value-to-free-cash-flow ratio has outperformed a similar strategy using forward P/Es by at least 2% since 1986, with less volatility.[6]

The problem with this statement is not the suggestion that cash flow is a better analytical tool when looking at an individual company (it is) but that it does not appear to be an apples-to-apples comparison. The analyst appears to be comparing the efficacy of using forward earnings to current cash flow—comparing a projection to actual. The real lesson is that deeper analysis is better. As discussed in earlier chapters, when looking at the entire market, operating earnings are used as a proxy for cash flow. P/E ratios for an individual company are useful as a rough guide, but you need to really understand the business in order to make an investment decision. As pointed out earlier, among other things, "E" does not adequately account for cash, minority interests, and other investments. One reason to use the P/E ratio when looking at individual companies is that E is standardized and widely available.

ALMOST NAILED IT

More than a year earlier, on March 3, 2009, just one week before the S&P 500 bottomed out, David Gaffen for the *Wall Street Journal* nailed it with, "To P/E or Not to P/E? That Isn't the Appropriate Question." Gaffen argues that focusing any valuation metric can be a mistake when earnings are so uncertain.

> *"Valuation is the wrong concept in a secular bear market,"* says John Mauldin, president of Millennium Wave Investments in Dallas. *"If we continue to see earnings drop from forecasted levels, as we have for over a year, then it is possible we could see more pain. Valuation is subjective in such a climate. When earnings start to stabilize, and we can get some visibility, then we can talk about fair value."*[7]

While he reached the right conclusion regarding earnings, he says that valuation is a wrong concept. It would have been better to say that you can't rely on P/E as a benchmark when there is so much uncertainty about E. The problem is not that P/E is a bad indicator; it is that you don't have a reliable estimate for E. It would have been better to offer a slightly more complicated explanation rather than risk leading the reader astray. Once again, be aware of oversimplifications.

GRAHAM AND DODD

Benjamin Graham and David L. Dodd, commonly referred to as Graham and Dodd, wrote a textbook in 1934 called *Security Analysis* (McGraw-Hill) that is still used today. They are considered the fathers of value investing. Warren Buffett took Graham's course at Columbia Business School in the 1950s and went to work for him before setting out on his own.[8] Most of what they advocated still makes good sense today, but one technique that has received attention recently is the selection of E in P/E. They suggested that earnings should be based on a 10-year average. The idea was to normalize earnings rather than take the most recent earnings to account for market cycles and one-off events. The approach received more attention when economist Robert Shiller published his book *Irrational Exuberance* (Princeton University Press, 2000) that made use of this method to show that the market was overvalued.

While the approach, sometimes called P/E 10, has some appeal, it also has some serious pitfalls. First, it does not account for interest rates, which, as we have seen, are an important driver of valuation. Second, by taking a 10-year historical average for earnings, it ignores much of the real growth that has occurred. Figure 10.1 illustrates the problem with this approach. The data are taken from the Robert Shiller's web site and show real earnings from 1871 through the present as sourced by Shiller. You can see that taking a 10-year average would give you an earnings figure much lower than the trend line for earnings, especially in recent years, where earning have grown

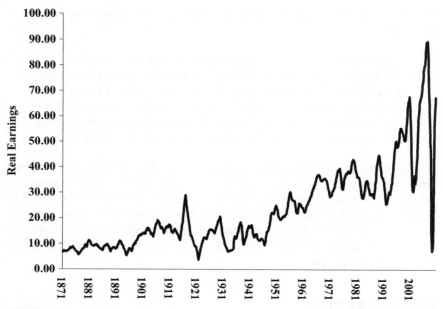

FIGURE 10.1   S&P 500 Annual Earnings (1871 to 2010)
Source: Earnings and inflation data from "Online Data Robert Shiller"
(www.econ.yale.edu/~shiller/data.htm); analysis by the author.

dramatically. The Graham and Dodd approach was created in the 1930s to
normalize earnings. In a period where earnings were not showing much real
growth, ignoring real growth might not be material. But given the higher
level of earnings growth in the past couple of decades, perhaps caused by
technology-driven gains in productivity, it seems clear that taking a 10-year
average considerably understates normalized E. Remember, Graham and
Dodd's intent was to normalize earnings, not to understate them.

On October 28, 2008, David Leonhardt wrote, "Are Stocks the Bargain
You Think?" for the *New York Times*. Clearly, they were not. The S&P
500 closed that day at 940. It still had another 30 percent to fall before
it bottomed out in March 2009. Leonhardt, along with many others, are
fans of Graham and Dodd. He explained the P/E 10 analysis and used it to
illustrate that stocks were not a bargain.

The argument is that since corporate profits can fluctuate, earnings
need to be normalized. Historically, this approach had seemed to be a good
indicator of overall valuation in the market. The long-term average for the
ratio was about 16, and when P/E 10 exceeds 20, the market has entered a
long-term decline.

After Tuesday's big rally, the ratio was just a shade below 16, or almost equal to its long-run average. This is a little difficult to swallow, I realize. Stocks are down 40 percent since last October, and every experience from the last 25 years suggests they now have to bounce back.[9]

While Leonhardt was right and stocks had a long way to fall, the fall was not due to the relative P/E 10 ratio, but due to the fact that earnings fell off a cliff. They dropped 39 percent over the next four quarters.

THE WRONG DISCUSSION

Nearly every day you can hear market sentiments on CNBC. While CNBC has a lot of great guests and commentary, some of it is of little value. For example, on the morning of November 30, 2010, the following comments were reported by one of the guests, who I will leave unnamed: "Although the market is a little weak, it's in a bottoming-out process technically," and "We'll get a bounce up to 1,250 before we really have the big decline that we've been expecting for some time."

He went on to offer little in the way of evidence through the rest of the interview. This kind of analysis offers no value and should be ignored; it can even be dangerous. Dangerous—how? If you have developed an independent point of view that the market, for example, may be overvalued, this type of argument may subconsciously reinforce your belief, causing you to hold the belief more strongly, but for no good reason. And, even worse, as your belief strengthens, you might be more likely to ignore evidence that contradicts your original belief.

DUMB MONEY AND BUBBLES

On August 21, 2010, an article titled, "In Striking Shift, Small Investors Flee Stock Market," appeared in the *New York Times*. Small investors were pulling out of the market in record numbers, having withdrawn more than $33 billion during the first seven months of 2010:

Now many are choosing investments they deem safer, like bonds. If that pace continues, more money will be pulled out of these mutual funds in 2010 than in any year since the 1980s, with the exception of 2008, when the global financial crisis peaked.[10]

The title of the article seems to suggest the need to feel alarmed. Is this really a sign of danger? The tone of this commentary suggests that this lack of confidence is a sign of further trouble ahead for equities. In fact, the research indicates the opposite. "Dumb Money: Mutual Fund Flows and the Cross-Section of Stock Returns," a 2006 paper by Andrea Frazzini (University of Chicago) and Owen A. Lamont (Yale), if not obvious from the title, concludes that money flow is a contraindicator. Excess money flowing in raises price and leads to an eventual market decline, while money flowing out tends to presage a rally. They put it simply:

> Our main result is that on average, retail investors direct their money to funds which invest in stocks that have low future returns. To achieve high returns, it is best to do the opposite of these investors. ... We call this predictability the "dumb money" effect.[11]

A similar sentiment was expressed by Joan Lappin of Gramercy Capital in *Forbes* in an article titled, "Bond Lemmings Headed for the Cliff."[12] She compares the bond market in 2010 to the 2000 tech bubble and points out that the flows into bond funds "dwarf whatever led to the bubble in 2000 by a long shot." The "dumb money" was flowing out of equity funds and into bond funds. The lesson is that following the crowd is often a bad strategy. It is important to think and develop your own point of view. Read the commentary with a critical eye and dig deeper.

THE RIGHT DISCUSSION

James Altucher wrote "The Bears Are Dead Wrong" for his financial advisors column in the *Wall Street Journal* on March 16, 2010. Tired of an endless flood of e-mails from market bears, he responded to their arguments. Most of the points were directly related to the overall prospects for a strengthening economy, referencing foreclosures, stimulus, and inflationary pressures from the Fed's "printing money. " He argued that while homes were still being foreclosed, the trend was positive; while unemployment was still 10 percent, the underlying trends point to recovery; and while the stimulus may not have worked, it really was not important to begin with.

Even though his arguments were a bit dismissive of legitimate concerns, he was clearly focused on items that ultimately impact interest rates and earnings; this is where you should be focused if you are trying to gauge opportunities in the stock market. As we know from the RPF Model, earnings growth is good, and higher inflation, which drives interest rates, is bad for valuation. For the purpose of this discussion, it does not matter what his arguments were and whether he was right or wrong; the important thing is that he is talking about the right things. When you are evaluating the market value, these are the conversations you need to pay attention to. Altucher distinguished himself further by slapping down those who argued that P/E ratio might return to 1970s' and 1980s' era levels.

> *Market timers often point to the lows in the '70s or early '80s when P/E ratios hit as low as seven and the market burst forth from there. Unfortunately for them, there is no hard and fast rule about what P/E ratios should be. If you flip over the P/E ratio so you get E/P you get the earnings yield of a company. The key is to compare earnings yields with the interest rates on products with comparable risk (corporate bonds, for instance). Interest rates were in double digits in the early '80s, so P/E ratios had to be much lower to compete.*[13]

And that's the point of this chapter: when trying to determine if the market is under- or overvalued, focus on the drivers of valuation—earnings and interest rates.

CHAPTER RECAP

Headlines don't always capture the nuances of the story. Market commentary should be interpreted through the lens of the RPF Model. Before taking it seriously, commentary must be analyzed carefully because the raw commentary can be oversimplified and potentially misleading. If the analyst does not support his or her statement with fundamentals, such as earnings, interest rates, or economic activity, ignore them. It is also worth remembering that being overly conservative can be as dangerous to your wealth as taking excessive risks.

CHAPTER 11

Using the RPF Model for Investment and Business Strategy

This chapter recaps the major points of the book, then applies the model and tools to investment analysis, including identifying and exploiting bubbles, investing in individual companies, applying the Risk Premium Factor (RPF) Model to business decision making, value destruction, and value creation.

The RPF Model exposes the elegant simplicity of valuation and highlights the importance of the factors that drive value. This chapter will highlight and summarize some of the value-creating approaches discussed in this book. Let's begin with a recap of the key elements of the RPF Model:

1. The equity risk premium (ERP) is not a constant but a stable factor applied to the risk-free rate (10- or 30-year Treasury yields)—the risk premium factor (RPF).
2. The RPF is consistent with the loss aversion coefficient associated with Prospect Theory (Kahneman and Tversky, 1979, 1992).
3. The Risk Premium Factor Valuation Model ($P = E/(R_f \times (1 + RPF) - (R_f - Int_{R} + G_R))$) effectively explains both price-to-earnings (P/E) ratio and Standard & Poor's (S&P) 500 Index levels using readily available information and simplifying assumptions.
4. By applying the current RPF and long-term assumptions for growth and real interest rates, it can be applied to predict current P/E and price of the S&P 500 and simplified to:
   a. $P = E/(R_f \times (1 + RPF) - (R_f - 2.0 \text{ percent}) + 2.6 \text{ percent}))$
   b. $P/E = 1/(R_f \times (1 + RPF) - (R_f - 2.0 \text{ percent}) + 2.6 \text{ percent}))$

5. Growth is a critical component of valuation; the impact of growth on value is easily quantified.
6. Interest rates drive market value—fair value of the market (P/E ratio) cannot be evaluated without considering interest rates.
7. Interest rates have a greater impact on market price and valuation than generally recognized—low rates are more beneficial and high rates are more punishing.
8. Declining interest rates were a major factor in the long bull market that began in the early 1980s.

ESTIMATING FAIR VALUE: HOW TO IDENTIFY AND EXPLOIT BUBBLES

One of the most direct uses of the RPF Model is to calculate intrinsic value of the S&P 500 and compare it to current market value. While the calculation is straight forward, application requires deeper analysis. The basic formulas are:

$$P = E/(R_f \times (1 + RPF) - (R_f - 2.0 \text{ percent}) + 2.6 \text{ percent}))$$

$$P/E = 1/(R_f \times (1 + RPF) - (R_f - 2.0 \text{ percent}) + 2.6 \text{ percent}))$$

Simply plug in the current risk-free rate to calculate P/E, and S&P 500 earnings to calculate intrinsic value of the index. The analysis comes in picking the right input variables. The current environment as this chapter is being written provides a good example of the underlying thought that is required.

Example: Estimated S&P 500 on December 1, 2010

You can get current bond yields from numerous sources, including Bloomberg (www.bloomberg.com/markets/rates-bonds/government-bonds/us/) and Yahoo Finance (finance.yahoo.com/bonds). On December 1, 2010, the yield on the 10-year Treasury was 2.95 percent. Getting S&P earnings takes a bit more work. As of this writing, they can be downloaded from the Standard & Poor's web site. These are the steps:

1. Go to www.standardandpoors.com/home/en/us.
2. Click on "S&P 500."
3. Expand the menu under "Download Index Data" by clicking the "+."

4. Click on "Index Earnings." This will download a spreadsheet (registration required).
5. The tab "ESTIMATES&PEs" has actual and forecast operating earnings by quarter; the tab "12 MONTH VALUES" has annual actual and forecasts.
6. Adding the most recent four quarters on the "ESTIMATES&PEs" tab gives you trailing 12-month earnings.

I typically use the most recently reported quarters along with the estimate for the current quarter. In this case they are the same, at $83.39. Plugging these figures into the RPF Model yields:

$$P/E = 1/(2.95 \text{ percent} \times (1 + 1.48) - (R_f - 2.0 \text{ percent}) + 2.6 \text{ percent}))$$

$$= 26.6$$

$$P = 26.6 \times 83.39 = 2,214$$

Since the index stood at just 1,206, either this was a huge opportunity or we need to examine our inputs. Let's revisit the inputs. We used 10-year Treasury yields as the risk-free rate because that had been the basis of the original research. In reality, the 30-year is a better measure since it is a longer-term rate that better captures inflation. In addition, we know that the Fed was buying bonds to keep rates low. This is further evidenced by the spread between the 10-year and 30-year, which, with the 30-year yielding 4.25 percent, was at 130 basis points (bps) or 44 percent greater—its largest spread ever. Historically, the average spread was just 20 bps or 4 percent. Since the 30-year yield also probably is depressed by the Fed's buying, I substituted the 30-year yield in the preceding calculations without discounting for the average historical spread. (You could make a case for using 96 percent of the 30-year if you believed that the 30-year was fairly priced.) The result was a P/E of 17.6 and a predicted level for the S&P of 1,466—about 20 percent above actual. Next, performing sensitivity analysis, we find that the risk-free rate would need to rise to 5 percent for the S&P 500 predicted to equal actual value. Now we are left with two key questions:

1. Do you believe current earnings are at least sustainable or might actually grow?
2. Do you believe yields will remain below 5 percent?

Given that at this point in time we were at the very early stages of recovery, my answer was yes. And only because my answer was "yes" did I believe there was buying opportunity. What if I believed the answer to the second question was "no" or "uncertain." In this case, I could hedge against rising rates by either selling short long-term Treasuries (not easy for an individual) or buying a fund that tries to mimic a short position in Treasuries.

Given the low prevailing long-term bond rates, many had called this a bond bubble. A bond bubble is not exactly like a stock or real estate bubble. If you bought a 10-year Treasury in September 2010 that yielded 2.75 percent with yields at 2.95 percent in December 2010, it lost some value, but you were still guaranteed to get your principal back along with interest payments. For example, if you bought $1,000 in 10-year Treasuries with a yield of 2.75 percent, you would be guaranteed to get your $1,000 back plus $27.50 per year in interest. It's risk free from the standpoint of returning your principal plus interest at a guaranteed rate. But it's not completely risk free because if interest rates rise, the value of the bond falls. Let's say yields rise back to 5 percent; then, the value of your $1,000 bond will fall to about $826. While you will still get your guaranteed payments and principal back at the end of 10 years, if you wanted to sell your bond, you would take a loss of about 18 percent. Another way to think of this is that you lost the opportunity to receive interest of $50 per year instead of your guaranteed $27.50. This could be considered a bond bubble because bond prices appear to be highly inflated.

Taken together with low equity prices, you might consider 2010 to be an inverse bubble. Past bubbles, such as 1987, were caused by rising interest rates caused by inflated equity values relative to both earnings and the risk-free rate. If you flip back to Figure 4.2, the outline of the bubble is clear. The ideal strategy would have been to be long Treasuries and short equities or at least move the bulk of your portfolio from equity to bonds. In 2010, the opposite appeared to be true; in a bond bubble, investors should not have any long-term bond exposure and should be long equities.

As you can see, the strategies for dealing with or exploiting a bubble are simple. Once you identify it, exit the investment that is overvalued and buy the ones that appear undervalued. While this sounds very much like "buy low and sell high," the difference is that the RPF Model gives you the tools to evaluate when the price is high or low. The good news and the bad news is that bubbles take some time to play out. Measured as the time from when actual begins to significantly deviate from predicted to the time when they return to parity, the 1987 bubble was 13 months and the 2000 bubble was 23 months. This is good news because you have time to determine that you are in a bubble, but bad news because you might need to be patient and perhaps brave while you wait for it to play out. Another note of caution: reaching parity does not guarantee good returns. In 2000, the actual and predicted reached parity in March 2000, but the market kept declining as earnings continued to fall, and then 9/11 hit; finally, war in Iraq contributed to the RPF's shifting higher and further driving valuations downward.

Closing a Valuation Gap: September 2010 to February 2011

In late September 2010, the market appeared undervalued and Treasury yields were low and appeared overpriced. The result was a large gap between predicted and actual value of the S&P 500. As discussed earlier, bubbles in 1987 and 2000 were partially driven by the market's slow response to climbing Treasury yields. At this time, the opposite appeared to be true. In an article on September 28, 2010, on SeekingAlpha.com, explaining my predicted value for the S&P 500, I wrote:

> Today the model shows a similar but opposite condition in that equities appear to be greatly underpriced [and bonds overvalued.] In order to be conservative, I used a risk free rate of 4% which is above both the 10 and 30 year Treasury rates. For earnings, I simply used trailing twelve month S&P 500 operating earnings of about $80 per share. The result is a predicted S&P 500 Index of 1,505—about 30% above its current 1,142.
>
> While the market has in the past returned to the levels suggest by the model, it is not always, by price adjustments. This could mean that earnings are set to fall or interest rates rise. ..."

The full text of this article is included in Appendix C. Alternatively, using the formula from Chapter 6 (Risk-Free Rate (R_f) = (E/P − Int$_R$ + G_R)/RPF), the implied risk-free rate (30-year yield) was 5.1 percent. As it turns out, interest rates began to rise along with the S&P 500 Index.

I continued to track this convergence in another article where, despite some concern the market was overvalued, I suggested that it still had room to run (Appendix D). Finally in early February, I documented the completion of the convergence (Appendix E), "30% Value Gap in S&P 500 Closed by Rise in Treasury Yields, Price" The convergence is illustrated in is shown in Figure 11.1.

Table 11.1 shows that movement in interest rates is the biggest factor that drove convergence.

The rise in yields combined with a 15 percent increase in the S&P caused predicted and actual to converge by mid-February 2011. This is an important lesson. When confronted with seemingly anomalous data or results, something had to give. Either the model was wrong or the factors

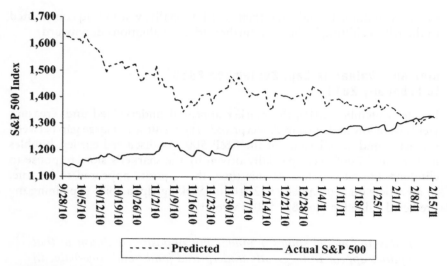

FIGURE 11.1 Predicted and Actual Converge—Late 2010 through Early 2011
Sources: S&P earnings and price from 1988 to present from Standard & Poor's web
site (www.standardandpoors.com/indices/sp-500/en/us/?indexId=spusa-500-usduf–
p-us-l–); Treasury yields from Federal Reserve, H.15 Selected Interest Rates
(www.federalreserve.gov/datadownload/Choose.aspx?rel=H.15). Because earnings
are released quarterly, the model was extended to monthly and daily price data by
using operating earnings as a constant for each month in the quarter applied for the
month preceding quarter end (i.e., December to February = Q1) under the
assumption that market expectations would have incorporated earning
expectations. Calculations and methodology by the author.

TABLE 11.1 Drivers of Convergence—Late 2010 through Early 2011

	28-Sep-10	31-Dec-10	15-Feb-11
30-year Treasury	3.7%	4.3%	4.7%
S&P Operating Earnings	79.02	83.94	83.94
S&P 500 Actual	1,147	1,257	1,328
S&P Predicted	1,641	1,441	1,333
% Difference	43%	15%	0%

Source: S&P earnings and price from Standard & Poor's web site (www.
standardandpoors.com/indices/sp-500/en/us/?indexId=spusa-500-usduf–p-us-l–);
Treasury yields from Federal Reserve, H.15 Selected Interest Rates (www.
federalreserve.gov/datadownload/Choose.aspx?rel=H.15). Calculations and methodology by the author.

were set to change. The key to applying the model lies in assessing the inputs and applying appropriate factors.

These examples illustrate how the RPF Model can be used as a predictive tool. The articles illustrate my thought process in analyzing the situation at the time, without benefit of hindsight. In this case, the model clearly showed that S&P 500 Index was undervalued relative to Treasury yields and current earnings, but could isolate the cause. Since earnings appeared reasonable, the cause of the divergence could be narrowed to either index price or Treasury yield as the cause. As it turned out, the gap between predicted and actual was closed in equal parts by a rise in yield and increase in price of the index.

BEWARE OF RPF SHIFTS

As discussed in Chapter 2, the RPF can shift. It shifted in 1981 and in 2002, both in response to major economic events. Surprisingly, it did not appear to have shifted during the 2008 to 2009 crisis—as we've seen it still explains the market. The fact that the past shifts were 20 years apart does not mean it will shift every 20 years. It is an important number, and you need to be aware that it can change. A shift in the RPF can cause it to appear that either a bubble has formed or a buying opportunity is present when the deviation of predicted from actual values was actually caused by the RPF shift. For example, in mid-2002 the market appeared to be significantly undervalued, when the RPF had actually jumped from 0.90 to 1.48. It was not clear that this was a permanent shift until later. However, as described in Chapter 2, an analysis of events at that time, including enactment of Sarbanes-Oxley and the start of the war in Iraq, could have provided a clue.

INVESTING IN INDIVIDUAL COMPANIES

Investing in individual companies is not for dilettantes. Professionals who manage investment funds spend huge amounts of money to learn about their targets. These are smart people who are paid well to do nothing but study companies. In order to compete, you need to do some work. When it comes to evaluating individual companies, the RPF Model does not provide absolute answers, but helps identify opportunities where companies may be mispriced relative to the market or peers and suggests where further analysis can be leveraged.

It is ironic that executives will spend a huge number of hours analyzing (or directing their subordinates to analyze) relatively small investments, yet manage their portfolios without having nearly the same level of diligence.

Sometimes reading a favorable article in the financial press may lead to a buy order. For example, a wealthy individual with a $5 million net worth might think nothing of making a $5,000 investment—0.1 percent of his or her net worth—in a publicly traded company. The same person responsible for a $1 billion market-cap business might cause his subordinates to labor over a $250,000 investment that represents just 0.025 percent of corporate assets.

My point is that it should not be surprising that using the RPF Model to evaluate individual companies takes work. As we've seen, trying to use the RPF Model to determine the stock price for an individual company does not make sense because the only way to estimate a meaningful long-term growth rate is by creating a multiyear forecast. Nevertheless, the RPF Model is a very useful as a tool to evaluate comparative growth expectations. As seen in Chapter 6, deriving the real implied growth rate (RIGR) shows market expectations for long-term growth implied in an individual firm's stock price. Comparing RIGR for a single firm to the overall market and its industry can help identify over- and undervalued firms and sectors. One approach discussed in Chapter 6 for understanding the relative expectations is to evaluate a company's RIGR relative to the entire S&P 500 Index by establishing percentiles. For example, if the average RIGR for the market is 1 percent, a 2 percent RIGR might indicate that investors expect the company to grow faster than the market and put a company in the upper 65 percent. This helps frame a series of questions:

- Does the company have enough growth prospects so that it can grow faster than the market in the long term?
- Can it maintain its competitive advantage?
- Will competition or new entrants threaten the core business or margins?

On the other end of the spectrum, consider a company that has an RIGR of −0.5%. In this case, the market expects earnings to decline over time. If you believe the company can maintain its position or even grow, it might present a buying opportunity.

REPORTED EARNINGS CAN BE MISLEADING

While reported operating earning do an excellent job at evaluating the market overall, and most individual companies, in some cases they can be terribly misleading. Accounting earnings are not always a good indication of value. While companies like Enron and WorldCom come to mind as examples of companies where distorted accounting earnings vastly overstated profitability, accounting earnings can also significantly understate true financial performance. Equity analysts routinely attempt to adjust accounting earnings to better understand true performance, while approaches like Economic Value Added are specifically focused on adjusting earnings and creating realistic measures of value creation.

On January 25, 2011, I published "Making the Case for Salesforce.com Valuation" (Appendix E). Salesforce.com had been widely ridiculed as overvalued based on its P/E ratio of 234. The article made the case that reported earnings are not a good measure for Salesforce.com. Saleforce.com sells access to its software as an online service. This is called a Software-as-a-Service or SaaS business. Customers purchase subscriptions to the service. Accounting rules, quite reasonably, force Salesforce to recognize this revenue on a monthly basis, so revenue is recognized as the service is delivered. The distortion comes on the cost side.

While customers may only commit to short-term contracts, say one-year, in reality after an initial trial, customers usually continue to subscribe to the service for many years. The expected value of this relationship is referred to as customer lifetime value or LTV. If customer on average are expected to to subscribe to the service for 10 years, then a customer with annual revenue of $100,000 actually has an expected LTV of $1 million. (While Salesforce does not report this number, they certainly know it internally.) As a result, with a high LTV, you would expect that they would spend aggressively on sales and marketing in order to secure new customers with this kind of expected annuity revenue stream. And they do.

The article shows how Salesforce.com is actually taking all of its new revenue and investing it back in the business by growing its investment in sales and marketing. As long as the LTV is high, this strategy makes sense. While accounting rules often try to match revenues with expenses, in this case they do not. Salesforce.com is forced to incur all of its sales and marketing expense in the period that it is incurred, despite the fact that the revenue may be many years off. This conservative approach is mandated because, while the revenue is expected, it is still uncertain.

The end result is that as Saleforce.com grows, and reinvests its revenue in sales and marketing, it does not grow reported earnings. In fact, until they take their foot off the gas and stop reinvesting in sales and marketing expense, they won't show much in the way of earnings. While the company would appear to be creating significant value, reported earnings do not reflect the value creation. Many analysts and investors understand this and reward Salesforce.com with share price increases as it grows revenue.

The article illustrates one method of understanding this valuation by projecting the growth rates in revenue and sales and marketing that justify the current sales price, then considering whether these growth rates are reasonable. Other approaches not discussed in the article are also appropriate.

One other approach would be to estimate a normalized sales and marketing expense that would allow Salesforce.com to maintain its current revenue and grow at a slower rate, then calculate earnings on this pro-forma basis. The pro-forma earnings multiples could be evaluated for reasonableness. A variant on this approach is to project several year of growth, and then calculate the terminal value based on a normalized sales and marketing expense level like we did in the mobile application example.

Yet another approach would be to capitalize sales and marketing expense and amortize it over the expected customer lifetime. This approach treats sales and marketing like the investment that it is and matches the expense with future revenues.

While none of these approaches is perfect, they each help better understand the true value of the underlying business.

HOW TO APPLY THE RPF MODEL TO DAY-TO-DAY BUSINESS DECISIONS

The RPF Model can be an important tool in day-to-day communication and decision making. By demonstrating that the simple constant growth equation explains stock market value, managers can understand and believe that if their decisions have the expected operating outcome in terms of growth and earnings, then market value will follow. The constant growth equation is a good tool for illustrating how earnings impact value and sustained growth is rewarded.

$$P = E/(C - G)$$

As you saw in Chapter 5, with the constant growth equation, if C and G are held constant, then price increases or decreases with E. A dollar of earnings derived from revenue growth can benefit both the top and bottom of the equation by demonstrating the ability to sustain growth, while a dollar from cost savings would be viewed as a one-time event that does not impact growth. I suspect that one reason executives may sometimes feel they are not being rewarded by investors is that they underestimate investor savvy. If a company grew earnings but revenues were flat, it would be reasonable to conclude that growth will slow. The result might be a lower P/E and a decline in stock price, resulting not from a lack of investor love, but investors' expectations that slowing growth offsets short-term gains in earnings. For the same reason, when a company misses earnings estimates, its stock price often declines. It is easy to see why. Price declines because earnings are lower and because of a reduction in the P/E ratio caused by the lower growth expectations implied by the lower-than-expected earnings.

CAPITAL STRUCTURE AND RISK IMPACT COST OF CAPITAL

Cost of capital also impacts value. By pursuing strategies that decrease the cost of capital, a company can increase value. Two factors that are somewhat in the control of senior leadership that impact the cost of capital are capital structure and risk. While providing a detailed game plan for executing strategies to impact cost of capital is beyond the scope of this book, it is worth a brief discussion. First, reducing risk should result in a lower beta, leading to a lower cost of equity. Theoretically, this can be done by reducing the volatility of earnings or decreasing leverage (lower debt). Acquiring a business with a different risk profile could also change the acquirer's beta, but could also alter growth expectations. Second, the weighted average cost of capital (WACC), which includes both debt and equity, can be lowered by a company with little debt taking on more debt. While the increase in debt would also increase beta, the debt tax shield from the deductibility of interest still results in a lower cost of capital. Conversely, a company with a high debt load may lower its cost of capital by deleveraging (reducing debt). The lowest theoretical cost of capital is called the optimal capital structure—the sweet spot that balances all these factors. A company with no debt can lower its cost of capital by replacing equity in its capital structure with debt. This can be executed by borrowing and then repurchasing shares or paying a large dividend.

The two key points to take from this discussion of cost of capital are:

- Being debt free is not optimal from a cost of capital perspective. The cost of capital can be lowered by taking on debt.
- Business mix impacts beta and thus cost of capital. Shifting to a riskier business could increase cost of capital.

OPPORTUNISTIC ADJUSTMENTS TO CORPORATE CAPITAL STRUCTURE

The period in late 2010 presented an opportunity for corporations to make substantial changes to their capital structure in the form of leveraged recapitalizations. Given the apparent low cost of debt and undervalued equity for the entire market, corporations had an opportunity to issue low-cost debt and use the proceeds to repurchase potentially undervalued shares. The shares could have been repurchased on the open market or through a tender offer.

For example, referring back to Figure 11.1 and Table 11.1, in late 2010 it seemed clear that the relative pricing of Treasuries to equities had created an unusual opportunity to issue debt. Predicted levels of the S&P 500 were very high, based on prevailing Treasury yields, and were still well above the actual index when yields were adjusted upward. This created a situation where not only was debt issuance very attractive but equities appeared undervalued. Companies that were able to issue debt at attractive spreads over Treasuries could also have repurchased their undervalued shares.

As discussed earlier, this would have the added benefit of lowering the cost of capital. At other points in time, when equities appeared expensive and yields were high, companies could have taken advantage of opportunities to deleverage by issuing new shares to retire debt. Late 1999 appeared to be an especially attractive time to issue equity. The RPF Model showed that the predicted level was more than 30 percent lower than actual in December 1999 and in the range of 20 to 30 percent below actual from April 1999 to August 2000 (see Figure 4.3). The rise in interest rates during 1999, which drove down the predicted value for the S&P 500, would have also driven down the value of fixed-rate debt, allowing some companies to repurchase their debt at less than face value. This could have been financed by the issuance of new shares. These periods are obvious in hindsight. The RPF Model has shown the ability to help identify these opportunities in real time, when they can be acted on.

CREATING A SENSE OF URGENCY

Significant bubbles (or inverse bubbles) are relatively rare events that create potential windows of opportunity that need to be acted on before the window closes. If you are in a transaction-oriented business like investment or commercial banking, the RPF Model is useful in not only identifying those windows but exploiting them. Getting clients to act often requires creating a sense of urgency. The RPF Model can be used to clearly communicate the magnitude of the opportunity. For example, as illustrated above, late 2010 was one of those rare windows where the relative pricing of Treasuries to equities had created an unusual opportunity to issue debt. By demonstrating the rarity of these windows and quantifying the opportunity, the RPF Model can also help create the urgency to act.

AVOIDING VALUE DESTRUCTION

There are many ways to destroy value, but at the top of the list is making bad investments. Knowing that its business is valued by a simple formula, $P = E/(C - G)$, management might be tempted to try and game the system by acquiring a company with high earnings but a low P/E in hopes that the acquired earnings will be valued at the acquirer's higher P/E. It does not work this way, and the constant growth equation can be used to demonstrate what really happens.

Let's assume we have two companies, acquirer and target. The acquirer has a cost of capital of 12 percent and a P/E of 20, while the lower-growth and lower-risk target has a cost of capital of 10 percent with a P/E of 10. Using the constant growth formula, where $P/E = 1/(C - G)$, we calculate implied growth of 7 percent for the acquirer and zero for the target. Table 11.2 shows this result, along with share price, shares outstanding, and market value for the two companies.

As you can see, both companies have the same market value, so this is a merger of equals. What do you think happens if the target is acquired for $80 per share, with the acquirer's earnings increasing from $100 million to $300 million? The new company does not get valued at a P/E of 20 or even a P/E of 15; the new company gets valued at a P/E of 13.33. Value does not get created out of thin air.

By viewing the combination through the lens of the RPF Model, it is easy to understand what happened. First, we calculate the number of new shares the acquirer must issue to complete the deal. Since we know the market value of the target is $2 billion, we calculate that the acquirer must issue 50 million new shares at the current price of $40, for a total of 100 million

TABLE 11.2 Acquirer and Target P/E Example

	Acquirer	Target
Cost of Capital	12%	10%
Growth	7.0%	0.0%
P/E	20.00	10.00
EPS	$2.00	$8.00
Share Price (M)	$40.00	$80.00
Shares Outstanding (M)	50	25
Total Earnings (M)	$100	$200
Market Value (M)	$2,000	$2,000

TABLE 11.3   Combined Value

	Acquirer	Target	Combined
Shares Outstanding (M)	50	25	100
Total Earnings (M)	$100	$200	$300
EPS	$2.00	$8.00	$3.00
Cost of Capital	12%	10%	11%
Growth	7.0%	0.0%	3.5%
P/E	20.00	10.00	13.33
Share Price (M)	$40.00	$80.00	$40.00
Market Value (M)	$2,000	$2,000	$4,000

shares in the combined companies. Next, we add the earnings for both companies together for a total of $300 million. Earnings per share (EPS) is $300 million divided by 100 million shares or $3 per share. This is all shown in Table 11.3.

For the new growth rate and cost of capital, we should not assume the combined company takes on the characteristics of the acquirer. It's like conservation of matter in physics—no alchemy takes place. The cost of capital for the new company is 11 percent because it is comprised of two equal parts, one at 12 percent and one at 10 percent. (If they were not equal, the combined cost of capital would be the weighted average.) The same is true of growth rate. By virtue of combining the two companies, the old zero growth part is not magically transformed into a growth machine. The new growth rate for the target is 3.5 percent; again, since it is equal parts 7 percent and zero, simply take the average.

Now it should become obvious what happens to the combined P/E ratio; it drops significantly. Using the constant growth equation, we see the P/E = 1/(C − G), so the new P/E = 1/(11 percent − 3.5 percent) = 13.33, and the combined share price stays at $40. Alternatively, by taking the new total market value of $4 billion and dividing by earnings of $300 million, we arrive at the same P/E of 13.33. Like conservation of matter, value is also conserved, as the combined market value is still $4 billion. Unless something happens to change the two companies, conservation of value applies.

What if the acquirer offered a premium? Let's say the acquirer offered a premium of 20 percent based on the stock price of each company to the announcement with the acquirer issuing 60 million (up from 50 million) shares to the target. Because the intrinsic value of each company is unchanged, we can assume that the cost of capital and growth rates remain the same; the only thing that changes is the number of shares.

The total number of shares for the combined companies is now 110 million, so EPS drops to $2.73. Since the P/E does not change, market value is still $4 billion for the combined companies, but the share price drops to $36.36 from $40 because there are now more shares outstanding. As a result, the original shareholders of the acquirer saw the value of their holdings drop from $2.0 billion to $1.8 billion, while shareholders of the target saw their holding increase to $2.2 billion. Once again, we see conservation of value, with the original shareholders losing value and the target gaining an equal amount of value, but total value is unchanged. There are a number of ways we could have analyzed this to derive the same result; my point here is to show that by correctly applying the RPF Model, you should reach the same conclusion.

Another way to destroy value is by investing in projects that don't provide a return in excess of the cost of capital. Instead of pursuing the acquisition above, let's suppose the company has $100 million in cash that is not earning any return, so it decides to invest it in a project that earns $5 million per year. Since this is only a 5 percent return and below the cost of capital, we should expect that it would destroy value. Using the constant growth equations, we see that $5 million with no growth at a 12 percent cost of capital ($5 million/(12 percent − 0 percent)) is worth only $45.7 million. Since we know that the value of equity is equal to the value of operations plus cash less debt, we know that by adding $45.7 million to our value of operations, while reducing cash by $100 million, destroys $54.3 million in value.

VALUE CREATION

Value is created by employing strategies that provide returns that exceed the cost of capital. This can be accomplished by growing earnings in the short term, creating sustained long-term growth or valuable options for future growth. Revisiting the $100 million investment described above, if instead of being a no-growth proposition, we expected the $5 million to grow at 8 percent, then the value of the investment would be $125 million. Even though the short-term returns are below the cost of capital at just 5 percent, long-term growth makes this a value-creating investment.

The purpose here is not to suggest that you use the RPF Model in place of other methods of making investment decisions, but to illustrate its use in thinking about and simply communicating investment decisions, along with

TABLE 11.4 Acquisition with Synergy

	Acquirer	Target	Syn.	Comb.
Shares Outstanding (M)	50	25		110
Total Earnings (M)	$100	$200	$20	$320
EPS	$2.00	$8.00		$2.91
Cost of Capital	12%	10%		11%
Growth	7.0%	0.0%	3.0%	5.0%
P/E	20.00	10.00		16.67
Share Price (M)	$40.00	$96.00		$48.48
Market Value (M)	$2,000	$2,000	$1,333	$5,333

the fact that it is consistent with traditional discounted cash flow (DCF) analysis.

Now let's revisit the acquisition. In the preceding example, we assumed that by combining the two companies, operations were unchanged. Value was destroyed because the buyer paid a premium but did nothing to make the combined companies more valuable than they were separately. Value is conserved and, in this case, transferred from buyer to seller. The only way to change value is to do something that impacts E, C, or G. If the rationale for the acquisition is not to game earnings, but instead based on the assumption that the acquirer could improve the results of the target, then value can be created.

Assume that as a result of the acquisition the buyer could reduce operating cost in the target and also leverage its own distribution to continue to increase long-term growth in the target from zero to 3 percent. The added value is synergy. Table 11.4 shows the result, with the buyer paying a 20 percent premium in the form an additional 10 million shares. In addition to columns for acquirer and target, we have added a column for synergy. The new combined growth rate is 5 percent (the average of 7 percent and 3 percent), up from 3.5 percent, which increases the P/E to 16.67 from 13.33. As a result, the value of the combined increases from $4 billion to $5.33 billion as the stock price rises from $40 to $48.48.

This does not violate conservation of value, since value was created not by the financial combination, but by reducing cost and increasing growth. Value was created by increasing both E and G. Note that the value creation did not get split evenly between acquirer and target. Even with a premium, the value of acquirer shares increases by $424 million ($8.48 × 50 million), while the target company shares increase from $2 billion predeal to $2.93 billion postdeal.

KEY MERGER-AND-ACQUISITION VALUATION CONCEPTS

Chapters 7 through 9 discussed the application of the RPF Model to analysis of acquisitions. Briefly, the key points are:

1. Use the RPF to calculate the ERP in your cost of capital.
2. Select the right project time horizon.
3. Normalize final-year cash flow.
4. Use the RPF Model to calculate the terminal value.

INFLATION IS THE ENEMY OF VALUE

Some argue that inflation should not have an impact on equity values, since higher costs can be passed on in the form of higher prices, so on average, earnings growth should keep up with inflation. For this to be value neutral, you have to assume a constant ERP, where C and G increase in lockstep. The RPF Model shows that in the constant growth equation ($P = E/(C - G)$), if inflation increases, then C increases faster than G, so P falls. C increases quickly because $C = R_f + ERP$. While R_f increases directly with expectations, the ERP increases based on the RPF, so a 1 percent increase in inflation results in a 2.48 percent increase the C but only a 1 percent increase in G. Back in Chapter 3, Table 3.1 showed how this translates in P/E ratio. An R_f of 4 percent implies inflation of 3 percent, which yields an expected P/E of 18.8. If R_f increased to 6 percent, that implies inflation of 4 percent, which would drop the expected P/E to 12.1, for an overall drop in value of more than a third.

This huge drop results from a seeming small increase in inflation from 2 percent to 5 percent. The risk premium is not a constant because investors expect a proportionately higher return over risk-free; as inflation rises, they apply a greater discount to future earnings, resulting in a lower present value, which leads to a lower P/E multiple.

FINAL THOUGHTS

Showing that the RPF Model explains the price of the S&P 500 Index in turn demonstrates that valuation of the entire market or a single company can be explained by three things: E, C, and G (earnings, cost of capital, and growth). This is a powerful realization, since it pulls the covers off the mystery of the stock market and shows that stock market valuation is actually simple and easy to understand. While managers have long known that E, C, and G were important, many were skeptical that the market actually worked in any predictable way. Understanding that the market actually does behave this way provides enhanced clarity for communication and decision making by focusing development of strategy and internal communication around these three powerful levers. If managers believe that by pulling these levers, investors will ultimately notice and it will impact stock price, they will be more likely to focus their efforts on these things that matter and tune out the noise.

Mobile Apps:
The Wave of the Past[*]

M obile today is like the Internet in the 1990s, with relatively slow connections and limited browser capability. Just like the PC Web, improvements in mobile Web will bring down today's walled gardens. Apple (NASDAQ: AAPL) is not AOL but still has much to lose.

I have an iPhone 4 and I love it. I love apps, and I love the app store. Apps simply deliver an experience you can't get on the mobile Web. But this love is not meant to last.

It's understandable why many believe that apps are here to stay. Reportedly, 6.5 billion apps were downloaded from iTunes; that's 54 for every iPhone. The trend line is steeply upward, but I think the runaway success of mobile apps is because they fill a temporary void, and the use of mobile apps will decline.

MOBILE PAST—RIM MISSES THE NEED FOR APPS

To understand why, let's look at the past. Mobile apps have been necessary and viable since the first Blackberry. While Research in Motion (NASDAQ: RIMM) should have won the battle of the app, they missed the opportunity.

I cofounded a company call iTendant in 2000, acquired by Servidyne (NASDAQ: SERV) in 2004. We built a Web and mobile software as a service (SaaS) platform (although we did not call it SaaS back then) to manage service and maintenance in hotels and office buildings. For many reasons (although there was a mobile Web), it would not work for our purposes. So we wrote applications for the Blackberry as the mobile component.

---

[*]This article was originally published on SeekingAlpha.com on September 28, 2010.

Initially, we had no support from Blackberry; we even had to pay to be part of their developer program. They did not see how making the devices more useful could significantly expand their market, and since they could not generate revenue from our app, they never offered more than token marketing support in the form of brochures to hand out at trade shows.

Part of Apple's genius in the app store was the understanding that free apps not only made the devices useful but also drove herds for traffic to their app store.

MOBILE TODAY—THE NEED FOR APPS

Apps were needed in the past and are needed today, but in five years, maybe not so much. In August, Chris Anderson and Michael Wolff wrote "The Web Is Dead. Long Live the Internet" for *Wired* magazine. They contend that a lot of what we do on the Internet is not on the Web but in apps, and that trend is expected to continue.

However, they missed a key observation: the trend in mobile is largely just a replay of the trends in the early Web and pre-Web, where applications (once called software on PCs, now call apps on mobile) were built to overcome inherent limitations. For example, PointCast, mentioned in the article, overcame slow dial-up speeds by pushing content, while AOL also cached content. As Internet speeds increased and browsers gained capabilities, these approaches were no longer necessary.

Remember Microsoft (NASDAQ: MSFT) Outlook, probably the biggest PC app ever? As browser capabilities and network speeds evolved, stand-alone apps were less necessary. Today, PC apps are generally for only the most demanding applications, like games, spreadsheets, and word processing; and even those are moving to the Web. Big money is betting on migration to the Cloud to continue.

LOOK BACK TO SEE AHEAD—MOBILE WILL FOLLOW PC EVOLUTION

Even mobile Web banner ads look like 1997. Of course, we need apps today. Applications fill a void by providing richer functionality, caching, and pushing of content to overcome mobile's present-day limitations. But if I could get the same experience by just going to a bookmarked Web page, why would I bother with downloading and endlessly upgrading apps?

The iPhone apps that I use most frequently like the *New York Times* (NYSE: NYT), CNN (NYSE: TWX), the *Wall Street Journal* (NASDAQ:

NWS), the Weather Channel, Facebook, LinkedIn, Twitter, Yahoo (NAS-DAQ: YHOO) and Gmail, (NASDAQ: GOOG), also rank as the top PC web sites and my top destinations.

Just like the PC Internet's evolution was driven by faster computers to support better browsers and faster connection speeds, as mobile devices get more powerful and connection speeds increase, mobile's evolution should continue to follow the same evolutionary path. In perhaps just a few years, we may see a much smaller market for mobile apps. They simply won't be needed for most functions, so the growth will abate, then decline.

IMPLICATIONS—THE END OF WALLED GARDENS

Much has been made of today's reemergence of walled gardens created by Apple and Google because of their app stores. If you are in the media business, you need to continue developing new apps with innovative ways to connect with your audience. You can't let someone else fill that void. Today, apps help extend and retain your audience.

But you also need to prepare and even push toward a post-app world to take power back from the walled garden.

Just like the PC, I expect the rise of a good mobile Web to topple the walled gardens while creating a platform-agnostic environment that levels the playing field. In this scenario, the one with the biggest garden has the most to lose: Apple. The diminished importance of apps will reduce switching costs for consumers since they will simply need to log in to web sites rather than worrying about losing favorite applications in the transition to a new device. This would put price pressure on Apple and create an opportunity for others to take share.

Technology on the Horizon: What if Moore's Law Continues for Another 40 Years?[*]

Moore's Law says that computer power doubles for the same cost about every two years, implying rapidly falling cost, increased power, and proliferation. If this continues, the equivalent price of a $600 iPhone would be $18.75 in 2020, $0.59 in 2030, and overall power or cost improving 1 million times by 2050. How should we account for this possible scenario in our investment strategies and plan for potential impact? What products and services have good present potential but could be enormous if Moore's Law continues?

Intel (NASDAQ: INTC) cofounder, Gordon Moore, wrote an article for *Electronics* magazine in April 1965, describing his thesis that the number of transistors that can be placed on a chip will roughly double every two years—meaning that computing power also doubles. He saw that this could lead to some revolutionary advancements:

> *Integrated circuits will lead to such wonders as home computers—or at least terminals connected to a central computer, automatic controls for automobiles, and personal portable communications equipment.*
>
> Gordon Moore, *Electronics* magazine, April 1965

It is an amazing vision. He was still with Fairchild Semiconductor, and Intel would not be founded for another three years. I am sure it seemed preposterous. Even *Electronics* magazine poked fun at him, placing a cartoon (not shown) with the original article. (To view the original article and cartoon, go to www.scribd.com/doc/30176118/Cramming-More -Components-Onto-Integrated-Circuits-Gordon-E-Moore-1965-Article.)

---

[*]This article was originally published on SeekingAlpha.com on October 6, 2010.

I recently wrote an article, "Mobile Apps: The Wave of the Past," which generated some good discussion about how mobile computing capabilities might be expected to progress. It reminded me of the importance of looking at the technology on the horizon—an important lesson that I learned in a consulting job interview during business school. The interviewer asked me an open-ended question about the future of the PC and how that might impact a particular company. I described at length what was happening at present. When I was finished, he paused, waited, and said, "You need to look at technology in terms of what is coming, not just what is." I didn't get the job but learned a powerful lesson. While present technology is important, you also need to look ahead. Easier said than done.

Just five years ago, how many people predicted that Apple (NASDAQ: APPL) would be poised to become the world's most valuable company by producing an affordable, powerful, connected pocket computing device? Looking back, the signs were there. Twenty years ago Apple made the Newton, 10 years ago we had Blackberries and Pocket PCs, and the first iPod in 2001. Just put these things together and extrapolate.

It's just not that easy. In 1943, Thomas Watson, chairman of IBM and no slouch in terms of technology vision, was famously reported to have said, "I think there is a world market for maybe five computers." His thinking was somewhat logical. In 1943 there just was not that much computing going on, so five computers ought to satisfy the market. Obviously, one missing piece here was that the availability of computing power would create demand, and falling prices would cause that demand to continue to grow.

Intel has been able to keep up with the pace predicted by Moore the past 40 years. What if this pace continues for the next 40 years?

The table below shows the projected relative computing power if Moore's Law continues at its current pace:

Year	Relative Computing Power
2010	$1\times$
2020	$32\times$
2030	$1024\times$
2040	$32,768\times$
2050	1 million $\times$

If this technological progress continues for another 40 years, computing hardware in 2050 will be more than 1 million times more powerful than today. And that's building on a base that already seems amazingly advanced.

To put this in perspective, if someone in gave you a penny in 1970 and its value doubled every two years like Moore's Law, today you'd have over $10,000—a nice return, but not life-changing money. If you could give that $10,000 to your children and it kept doubling in value every two years, in

40 years (2050) it would be worth more than $10 billion. Now we're talking real money.

From the computing power standpoint, we are sitting here marveling at the change that the first $10,000 has brought. What happens over the next 40 years when it turns into $10 billion? My point here is not to launch into my own futurist vision, but to suggest that as an investor or executive you need to think about how business and products might change based on massively falling cost and increased computing power. One way to approach the problem is by formulating questions based on this scenario.

While Moore's Law is often expressed and discussed in terms of power, it also has worked on the cost side of the equation. Every two years we get the same computing power for half the cost. Not only has this seemed to hold for Intel's chips but for other electronics as well.

In 1972, Hewlett-Packard (NYSE: HPQ) introduced its first pocket calculator, the HP-35, retailing for $495, about $2,600 in today's dollars. You can buy a scientific calculator today on Amazon (NASDAQ: AMZN) for $0.69 plus shipping. Basic calculators cost even less. Extrapolating Moore's Law from 1972, cutting the price by 50 percent every two years yields a projected price $0.005 today. Accounting for nonelectronic components, assembly, and shipping brings it close enough to make my point.

As another example, consider the Kindle. It was introduced in November 2007 for $399. A better model now retails for $189—a drop of more than 50 percent at retail in three years.

At this rate, a $600 iPhone without contract would be $18.75 in 2020 and $0.59 in 2020. The following table shows this extrapolation for iPhone and Kindle:

Year	iPhone	Kindle
2010	$ 600.00	$ 139.00
2020	18.75	4.34
2030	Less than $1.00	Less than $1.00

While Moore's Law applies specifically to integrated circuits, other components decline as well. As we've seen in a range of electronic equipment, from televisions to mobile phones, if you keep capabilities as a constant, prices drop like a rock. I am not categorically predicting that this will happen, but suggesting that this is a possible future scenario that requires exploration.

Computing power is the dimension many people usually think of with regard to Moore's Law. Each generation of desktop, laptop, and mobile give more power for the same price and size. Do we reach a limit where we just don't need any more power?

Similar to the progress in desktop publishing, home printing, digital photography, home video, and spreadsheets, all of which have been around for more than 20 years, but only became widespread with increases in computing power, what applications could exist that are not practical or at least just not good enough for primetime today?

I had Dragon Naturally Speaking for speech-to-text 10 years ago, but it was below adequate, required training, and was cumbersome to use. Occasionally, I use a much better version on my iPhone today. Can a voice interface all but replace the keyboard in the near future?

What happens to Google's (NASDAQ: GOOG) revenue if artificial intelligence improves search to the point that you get what you want on the first page with just one query?

These few examples are all visible today, and with a 32× improvement in computing power in 10 years or 1,000× in 20 years, seem within reach. What are the implications in 40 years with a possible 1 million times increase in computing power? What is made possible by having incredibly small but inexpensive and powerful hardware that can be everywhere and control anything electronic?

I understand that this is very complicated and Moore's Law does not impact the cost of software design, product design, capital cost for plants increases significantly, and batteries are not included. At the same time, I have not seen much written about how we might plan today to invest in products and services that leverage the possibility of Moore's Law continuing.

I am very interested in a dialogue on this. To seed the conversation, consider commenting with your thoughts on the following questions:

- What is the probability that Moore's Law will continue at pace for the next 10, 20, and 40 years?
- Where can very inexpensive but small and powerful computing be applied in the future?
- What is the impact on hardware manufacturers? (Apple, Dell [NASDAQ: DELL], Hewlett-Packard)
- Will massive benefits accrue to the companies that produce software and databases to harness this power? (Microsoft [NASDAQ: MSFT], Oracle [NASDAQ: ORCL])
- What is the impact on CPU manufacturers? (Intel, AMD [NYSE: AMD])
- Is there a limit to the need for computing power?
- What capabilities could exist with more power that are not practical or at least just not good enough for primetime today?
- What other implications in 40 years with a possible 1 million times increase in computing power for today's price?
- What products and services have good present potential but could be enormous if Moore's Law continues?
- What happens to Google's revenue if artificial intelligence improves search, and you get what you want more quickly?

A Simple and Powerful Model Suggests the S&P 500 Is Greatly Underpriced[*]

The Risk Premium Factor (RPF) Model can help understand the S&P 500's valuation to identify bubbles and opportunities. It is built on a simple constant growth equation where: P = E/(C − G) and explains S&P Index levels with good accuracy for 1960 to the present using only the risk-free rate, S&P 500 operating earnings, and some simplifying assumptions. Figure C.1 shows this relationship for the past 50 years.

This is based on a very simple model that can enhance understanding for investors by demystifying the factors that drive valuation.

The model shows that two factors drive the market:

1. Earnings
2. Interest rates, which drive cost of capital and embody inflation

And for individual companies, a third factor: Growth.

Understanding that these are the most important factors can help cut through much of the analytical noise to help investors focus on fundamentals.

This remarkably simple model has been useful in identifying the causes of past bubbles, and it continued to work through the recent financial crisis. More details follow below or read the full paper in the *Journal of Applied Corporate Finance* (http://papers.ssrn.com/sol3/papers.cfm?abstract_id= 1663812).

---

[*]This material was originally published on SeekingAlpha.com on September 28, 2010.

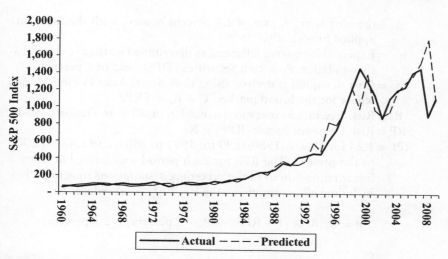

FIGURE C.1   S&P Historical Average (Actual vs. Predicted), Y/E Data 1960 to 2009

RISK PREMIUM FACTOR VALUATION MODEL

The constant growth equation, $P = E/(C - G)$, is a simple and well-known formula. The key to making this equation useful in valuation is deriving the variables. The most important innovation is that rather than using a fixed equity risk premium (ERP), I employ a new approach for estimating the ERP. Most approaches to deriving the ERP involve calculating a fixed spread between historical equity returns and the risk-free rate. The RPF model differs significantly in that the ERP is simply a function of the risk-free rate times a constant called the risk premium factor (RPF), where Equity Risk Premium = Risk Free Rate × RPF.

The remaining assumptions are summarized below:

P = Price (value of S&P 500).

E = Actual earnings (annualize operating earnings for the prior four quarters as reported by S&P). Earnings, while not ideal, are used as a proxy for cash flow and seem to work very well.

G = Expected long-term projected growth rate, which is broken down into real growth and inflation, so $G = G_R + I_{LT}$.

G_R = Expected long-term real growth rate. Long-term expected real growth rate (G_R) is based on long-term gross domestic product (GDP) growth expectations on the basis that real earnings for a broad index of large-cap equities will grow with GDP over the long term. A rate of 2.6 percent is used, with the same rate applied historically.

I_{LT} = Expected long-term inflation, as determined by the average Treasury Inflation-Protected Securities (TIPS) yield of 2 percent.

C = Cost of capital is derived using the Capital Asset Pricing Model, where for the broad market, $C = R_f + ERP$.

R_f = Risk-free rate as measured using 10- or 30-year Treasury yields.

ERP = Risk Premium Factor (RPF) × R_f

RPF = 1.24 for 1960 to 1980; 0.90 for 1981 to 2001; and 1.48 for 2002 to the present. The RPF for each period was arrived at using a linear regression to fit the preceding assumptions to actual PE. Including all assumptions, the $P = E/(C - G)$ reduces to:

$$P = E/(R_f \times (1 + RPF) - (R_f - 2\ percent) - 2.6\ percent)$$

or

$$P/E = 1/(R_f \times (1 + RPF) - (R_f - 2\ percent) - 2.6\ percent)$$

Using the current RPF of 1.48, the only variables necessary to determine the market price-to-earnings (P/E) ratio is the risk-free rate, then add earnings to get the predicted level of the S&P 500 Index. Please note that even with just these two variables, you must apply a test of reasonableness. For example, during the heat of the financial crisis, historical earnings were not a good benchmark. I contend that today the 10-year Treasury yield is not a good benchmark for risk-free and the 30-year yield or higher should be used.

You can also see from the equation that the price has an inverse relationship with interest rates. As rates go up, P/E comes down, and vice versa. The RPF model suggests that the decline in risk-free rates since the early 1980s is responsible for declines in ERP and contributed significantly to the rise in the S&P 500, accounting for more than half of the growth in the S&P 500 since 1981.

The model explains stock prices from 1960 to 2009 with R-squared around 90 percent. A picture is worth a thousand words. The simplest way to comprehend the effectiveness of the model is to look at the graphs. Figure C.2 shows how the model has predicted P/E since 1960.

The full paper, and I will warn you it's long, has a number of additional graphs that illustrate quarterly and monthly performance, and uses the model to dissect the causes of the October 1987 crash and 2000 bubble, along with an overview of how the RPF model showed that we were in a bubble.

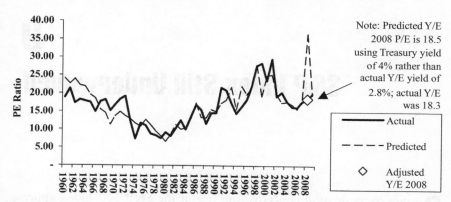

FIGURE C.2   S&P Historical P/E (Actual vs. Predicted), Y/E Data 1960 to 2009

WHAT IT MEANS TODAY

Today, the model shows a similar but opposite condition in that equities appear to be greatly underpriced. In order to be conservative, I used a risk-free rate of 4 percent, which is above both the 10- and 30-year Treasury rates. For earnings, I simply used trailing 12-month S&P 500 operating earnings of about $80 per share. The result is a predicted S&P 500 Index of 1,505—about 30 percent above its current 1,142.

While the market has in the past returned to the levels suggested by the model, it is not always by price adjustments. This could mean that earnings are set to fall or interest rates rise or that the model is wrong or the factors need to be recalibrated. Unfortunately, this uncertainty will always be the case in the midst of a bubble or inverse bubble.

When things begin to differ from past patterns, you hear rationalizations of the current condition. Remember, in early 2000, the talk of a new economy where old economy fundamentals no longer held was the rationalization for valuations. Today is the opposite, where instead the new economy is a pessimistic version of the old economy and old valuation metrics don't hold because of investor pessimism. In the past, it's taken a year for these aberrations in valuation to work themselves out. So within a year, we should know which is right.

In any case, the RPF Model is a very simple equation that helps cut through the noise to understand the drivers of valuation.

S&P Index Still Undervalued*

Despite overvaluation concerns, the rise in the S&P 500 Index appears to be earnings driven and not speculative. The Risk Premium Factor (RPF) Model shows that the S&P 500 is undervalued by about 7 percent, narrowing from the 30 percent undervaluation estimate that I reported in my September 28, 2010, article (see Appendix C) and the 20% that I reported on November 8, 2010. This suggests continued opportunities for investors, corporate buybacks, and mergers and acquisitions (M&A).

The narrowing of the gap was caused by rising Treasury yields, which drive down predicted levels coupled with an increase in the index. While continued increases in earnings in 2011 should be expected to drive the market higher, investors should keep a cautious eye on interest rates.

The RPF Model is built on a simple constant growth equation where:

$$P = E/(C - G)$$

This formula explains S&P Index levels with good accuracy for 1960 to the present using only the risk-free rate, S&P 500 operating earnings, and some simplifying assumptions. Figure D.1 shows this relationship since 1986.

Just as overvaluation during 1999 to 2000 is apparent in Figure D.1, recent undervaluation is also visible. For more background and graphs going back to 1960, you can read my summary of the RPF Model (Appendix C) or the full paper (http://papers.ssrn.com/sol3/papers.cfm?abstract_id= 1663812). Figure D.2 shows predicted versus actual price-to-earnings (P/E) ratios for the same period.

---

*This material was originally published on SeekingAlpha.com on January 6, 2011.

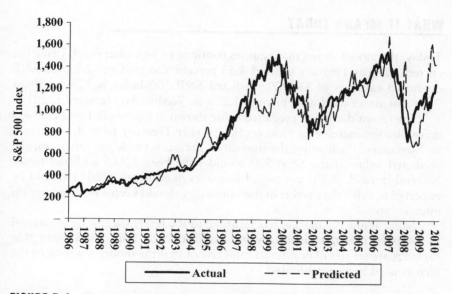

FIGURE D.1 S&P 500 Index (Actual vs. Predicted) Month-End Data 1986 to December 2010

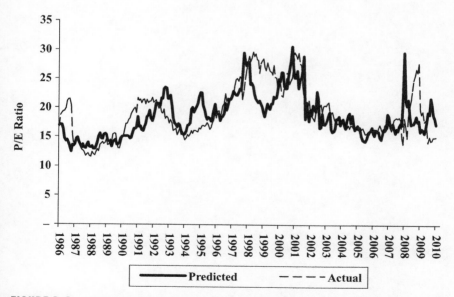

FIGURE D.2 S&P 500 P/E (Actual Vs. Predicted) Month-End Data 1986 to December 2010

WHAT IT MEANS TODAY

Today, the model shows that equities continue to be underpriced. Using the current 30-year Treasury yield of 4.55 percent and trailing 12-month S&P operating earnings of $83.67, predicted S&P 500 Index is 1,364—about 7 percent above its closing price of 1,276 on Wednesday, January 5, 2011.

The recent decline in predicted value shown in Figures D.1 and D.2 was driven by the increase in yield on the 30-year Treasury from 4.12 percent in November. Illustrating the impact of Treasury yields on valuation, the predicted value of the S&P 500 would have been 1,512 with the lower November yield. While continued increases in earnings in 2011 should be expected to drive the market higher, investors should keep a cautious eye on interest rates.

Note: While the market has returned to the levels suggest by the model in the past, it is not always by price adjustments. This could mean that earnings are set to fall or interest rates rise or that the model is wrong or the factors need to be recalibrated.

30 Percent Value Gap in S&P 500 Closed by Rise in Treasury Yields, Price*

When I first wrote about the Risk Premium Factor (RPF) Valuation Model on SeekingAlpha.com on September 28, 2010 (see Appendix C), I described how the S&P 500 appeared to be undervalued by about 30 percent based on expected 2010 earnings and current yield on 30-year Treasury bonds. The S&P 500 was at 1,142, and the 30-year Treasury was yielding 3.73 percent.

Because lower Treasury yields result in a higher predicted price in the model, I calculated the predicted level of the S&P 500 at 1,505, using a 4 percent yield to be more conservative. This still resulted in a large valuation gap, suggesting that the S&P 500 was undervalued by about 30 percent. I cautioned that in addition to a change in the price of the index, the gap could be closed by a changed in interest rates or earnings. The gap has closed—today, at 1,329, it looks like the S&P 500 is fairly valued with an intrinsic value suggested by the RPF Model of 1,315.

HOW DID THE GAP CLOSE?

The RPF Model bases predicted value on the risk-free rate as measured by Treasury yields and trailing operating earnings. The formula is: $P = E / (R_f \times (1 + RPF) - (R_f - 2\ \text{percent}) - 2.6\ \text{percent})$, where:

---

*This article was originally published on SeekingAlpha.com on February 12, 2011.

P = Predicted price (value of S&P 500 Index).

E = Actual earnings (annualize operating earnings for the prior four quarters as reported by S&P). Earnings, while not ideal, are used as a proxy for cash flow and seem to work very well.

R_f = Risk-free rate as measured using 10- or 30-year Treasury yields.

RPF = Risk Premium Factor, 1.24 for 1960 to 1980; 0.90 for 1981 to 2001; and 1.48 for 2002 to the present.

Since September 28, the S&P 500 is up about 16 percent. Earnings are also up 5 percent to $83.94 and the yield on the 30-year has jumped to 4.72 percent. As you can see from the preceding formula, when Treasury yields rise, the predicted value of the S&P 500 falls. The following table summarizes the impact of each factor that caused the predicted and actual values to converge:

Change in Predicted Due to Treasury Yields	−21%
Change Due to Earnings	6%
Total Change in Predicted	−15%
Actual Change in Index (9/28/10–2/11/11)	16%

As shown in the table, the biggest factor was the rise in Treasury yields that caused the predicted value of the index to fall by 21 percent, followed by a 15 percent rise in the S&P 500 Index, which accounted for the remainder of the convergence.

DEVELOPING YOUR OWN FORECAST

Since the index is highly sensitive to Treasury yields and earnings, future performance is dependent on these two factors. In order to develop your own set of expectations for the S&P 500 Index, you need to apply your view on these two factors to the model. You can use the preceding formula to calculate the predicted value of the S&P 500 based on your expectations or download my RPF Value iPhone app (available through iTunes) to perform the calculation based on your own inputs.

Based on expected earnings for 2011 of $92; the analyst average in my December 16, 2010, article (http://seekingalpha.com/article/242066-strategists-lowball-2011-projections-for-s-p-500); and a Treasury yield of 4.7 percent, the S&P would end 2011 at about 1,441, falling to 1,353 if the 30-year rises to 5.0 percent. You can use the calculator (available through iTunes) to perform these and other sensitivities to develop your own view of the market.

Making a Case for
Salesforce.com Valuation[*]

Numerous articles have criticized Salesforce.com (CRM), claiming that it is overvalued and represents clear evidence of a tech bubble. Most recently, an article entitled "Shades of the Dot-com Bubble" appeared in *Barron's* on January 22. With a stratospheric price-to-earnings (P/E) ratio of 234, how can it not be overvalued? Customer lifetime value (LTV), not P/E, is the key to understanding Salesforce.

Let's look at what it would take to justify a $200 share price today and then ask if it's reasonable. The bottom line is that if sales growth averages 26.1 percent; sales, general and administrative (SG&A) growth averages about 9 percent; and the terminal value P/E is 20, the company is worth $128.50 per share today.

One key factor that many analysts miss is that the software-as-a-service (SaaS) business model creates an annuity revenue stream, since customers pay an annual subscription to access the service. Implementing the software takes time, and switching to another provider is expensive. The switching costs increase over time, as each client accumulates historical data and processes become entrenched in the organization.

Salesforce, however, incurs high up-front customer acquisition costs but low ongoing expenses. A solid product combined with high switching costs yields excellent customer retention. Since each new customer is expected to remain for many years—and even grow as they add new seat licenses and expand services—customer LTV is very high. While Salesforce does not disclose retention rates, you can be sure it knows its LTV.

If we assume that, for every dollar Salesforce invests in customer acquisition, it expects years of revenue, it makes sense that it should be plowing all

---

[*]This article was originally published on SeekingAlpha.com on January 25, 2011.

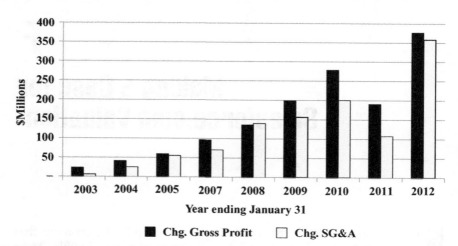

FIGURE F.1 Salesforce.com Change in Gross Profit versus Change in SG&A
Source: i-Metrix.com/Hassett Advisors Analysis.

of its profits back into customer acquisition. With a gross margin of about 81 percent, new revenue falls to the bottom line, so it's a great return on investment.

Looking at it another way, Salesforce strategy is to focus on growth at the expense of earnings. Figure F.1 shows the annual change in gross profit compared to the annual change in SG&A.

Gross profits are being used to ramp sales efforts. Unlike many other businesses, since we assume that each new customer generates revenue for many years without additional sales effort, if Salesforce were to cut its sales expense, revenues might plateau with very deep cuts—but would not fall. Sales costs are really an investment and not a cost. Unfortunately, the result of this strategy is that net income and earnings per share (EPS) remain low, so the P/E looks ridiculously high. If customer LTV is a multiple of acquisition cost, then this strategy makes sense because it drives long-term value. But even if the strategy is sound, it does not mean the company is not overvalued. For that, we need to look at the financials.

Absent a good basis for projecting long-term revenue growth, an alternative approach is to reverse-engineer to the stock price to see what it would take to support today's valuation, then explore the reasonableness of those assumptions (see Table F.1). To do this, I focused on three key drivers: revenue growth, SG&A expense, and exit multiple. I projected 2011, the current year, which ends on January 31, and used it as a basis for projections to see what it would take to justify today's price of $127.50 per share.

TABLE F.1 Salesforce.com (CRM) Year Ending January 31

$M	2011	2012	2013	2014	2015	2016
Revenue	1,662	2,095	2,642	3,332	4,201	5,298
Gross Profit	1,342	1,695	2,137	2,695	3,399	4,286
SG&A Total	1,025	1,115	1,214	1,322	1,439	1,568
R&D	182	200	220	231	243	255
Total Operating Expense	1,207	1,316	1,434	1,553	1,682	1,823
EBIT	140	379	703	1,142	1,717	2,463
PBT	149	379	703	1,142	1,717	2,463
Tax	57	140	254	406	603	860
Net Income	92	240	449	737	1,113	1,602
Diluted Shares (M)	134	137	140	143	146	149
EPS	0.68	1.75	3.20	5.15	7.62	10.74
Investment*	(38)	(48)	(61)	(77)	(97)	(122)
Cash Flow	54	192	388	660	1,017	1,480
Terminal Value						32,043
NPV Cash Flow	54	192	388	660	1,017	33,524
NPV	19,168					
Shares	149					
Intrinsic Share Price	$128.55					

*Capex, Deferred Commissions, Chg. Working Capital.

The bottom line is that if sales growth averages 26.1 percent, SG&A growth averages about 9 percent, and the terminal value P/E is 20, the company is worth $128.50 per share today.

Obviously, the value is very sensitive to these variables. If revenue grows at only 25 percent, then the price falls to $107, but if revenue grows at 31 percent, the value jumps to $200 per share. If we extend the projections for another five years, a revenue growth rate of 23 percent hits $200 per share. Revenue growth will be about 27 percent for the current year, which ends in about a week. That's up from 21 percent in 2010 (calendar 2009) after growing 44 percent in 2009 and never less than 50 percent before that. Certainly, strong performance is required to justify today's stock price, but it seems far from clear that this expectation is unreasonable.

While Salesforce has shown exceptional growth and is a cash machine in the waiting, it is not clear whether it can sustain this high level of growth while keeping customer acquisition costs in check. The question of overvaluation is not driven by today's P/E. The key questions that investors should be asking are related to driving and sustaining growth:

- What are the customer acquisition costs? How are they trending?
- What is customer lifetime value? How is it trending?
- What is customer retention? How is it trending?
- What are revenues per customer? How are they trending?

These are some of the key questions that need to be answered in order to determine if Salesforce can grow into its share price. Without answers or at least a solid point of view, you really can't make the case that the company is over- or undervalued, and thus would hardly seem to be evidence of a tech bubble.

Beta: Measure of nondiversifiable risk relative to the S&P 500 reflecting the correlation of returns for a stock with the S&P 500.

Comps: Short for comparables; a term used to describe a set of peer companies used as a comparison, often for the purpose of establishing valuation multiples, beta, margins, growth, or other financial metrics.

Consensus earnings: Reported expected level of earnings by a group of analysts.

Constant growth equation: $V = E/(C - G)$. Calculates the present value of a constant cash flow in perpetuity assuming constant cost of capital and growth rate.

Cost of capital (C): The required return to justify an investment or expected rate of return for an investment of similar risk.

Cost of debt: The effective rate a company pays on its debt.

Cost of equity: The return stockholders require for investing in a company; the risk-free rate plus a risk premium.

Discounted cash flow (DCF) analysis: Calculation of present of a stream of future cash flows used to evaluate the attractiveness of an investment.

Discount rate: Cost of capital used in DCF and PV analysis.

Earnings per share (EPS): Net income for a company divided by shares outstanding.

Enterprise value or total market value: The total value of a company, including equity, debt, minority interests, and preferred shares less cash and equivalents.

Equity risk premium (ERP): Return in excess of the risk-free (R_f) rate that the S&P 500 Index is expected to yield.

Forward P/E: P/E ratio based on consensus earnings.

Future comps: Comps based on the characteristics of the company at some future date.

Future value (FV): The value of money invested today at a future date at an assumed cost of capital.

Intrinsic value: The underlying or actual value of something, often used to denote the value calculated by an analyst as opposed to the actual market value or stock price.

Investment time horizon: Time period (i.e., number of years) over which you forecast cash.

Internal consistency: Consistency between assumptions in a financial model. For example, if the inflation rate in the cost of capital is 3 percent, the inflation rate in revenue projections also should be 3 percent.

Present value (PV): The discounted value of a promised future payment.

Risk-free rate (R_f):   A riskless or nearly riskless investment. For long-term investments, it is usually the 10- or 30-year Treasury yields.

Risk premium: Return in excess of the risk-free rate that an investment is expected to yield; premium to compensate investors for bearing risk.

RPF shifts: Changes in the risk premium factor; historically, an infrequent occurrence.

RPF or risk premium factor: Factor applied to risk-free rate (R_f) to determine equity risk premium (ERP). As of 2010, the RPF was 1.48.

RPF Model or Risk Premium Factor Valuation Model: RPF and simplifying assumptions for growth applied to the constant growth equation:

$$P = E/(R_f \times (1 + 1.48) - R_f + 2.0 \text{ percent} - 2.6 \text{ percent})$$

or

$$P/E = 1/(R_f \times (1 + 1.48) - R_f + 2.0 \text{ percent} - 2.6 \text{ percent})$$

where 2 percent is assumed long-term real interest rate and 2.6 percent is the assumed long-term real growth rate for the S&P 500.

S&P operating earnings: Reported earnings for the S&P 500 Index with certain charges reversed to exclude certain corporate or one-time expenses.

Terminal value: Value beyond the forecast horizon in a DCF analysis.

Terminal value multiple: Multiple applied to normalized terminal value cash flow to calculate terminal value

Total market value: See Enterprise value.

Weighted average cost of capital (WACC):   The cost of capital for a firm that weights the cost of equity with the after-tax cost of debt.

Notes

PREFACE

1. Eugene F. Fama and Kenneth R. French, "Luck versus Skill in the Cross Section of Mutual Fund Returns," *Journal of Finance* 65(5) (October 2010).
2. Standard & Poor's, Index and Portfolio Services, "Do Past Mutual Fund Winners Repeat? The S&P Persistence Scorecard," January 27, 2010. Available at SSRN: http://ssrn.com/abstract=1543364.
3. Stephen D. Hassett, "The RFP Model for Calculating the Equity Market Risk Premium and Explaining the Value of the S&P with Two Variables," *Journal of Applied Corporate Finance* 22(2) (Spring 2010): 118–130.
4. Justin Fox, *The Myth of the Rational Market: History of Risk, Reward and Delusion on Wall Street* (New York: Harper Collins, 2009), 199.
5. Daniel Kahneman and Amos Tversky, "Advances in Prospect Theory: Cumulative Representation of Uncertainty." *Journal of Risk and Uncertainty* 5 (1992): 297–323.
6. If this seems confusing, assume you have $100. If you choose to flip a coin, you end up with your original $100 plus your winnings, for a total of $325. If you lose, you have $0. If you don't flip, you are guaranteed to keep your $100.

CHAPTER 1

1. Paul Krugman, "Dow 36,000: How Silly Is It?," official Web page of Paul Krugman. November 2010 (http://web.mit.edu/krugman/www/dow36K.html).
2. Franco Modigliani and Merton H. Miller, "Dividend Policy, Growth, and the Valuation of Shares." *Journal of Business* 34(4) (1961); "The Sveriges Riksbank Prize in Economic Sciences in Memory of Alfred Nobel 1985," Nobelprize.org, November 16, 2010, http://nobelprize.org/nobel_prizes/economics/laureates/1985/; and "The Sveriges Riksbank Prize in Economic Sciences in Memory of Alfred Nobel 1990," Nobelprize.org, November 16, 2010, http://nobelprize.org/nobel_prizes/economics/laureates/1990/.
3. Shannon P. Pratt and Roger J. Grabowski, *Cost of Capital: Applications and Examples* (Hoboken, NJ: John Wiley & Sons, 2010).
4. Bradford Cornell, *The Equity Risk Premium: The Long-Run Future of the Stock Market* (New York: John Wiley & Sons, 1999).
5. Pratt and Grabowski, 2010.

171

6. Pablo Fernandez and Javier Del Campo Baonza, "Market Risk Premium Used in 2010 by Analysts and Companies: A Survey with 2,400 Answers," May 21, 2010. Available at SSRN: http://ssrn.com/abstract=1609563.

7. James K. Glassman and Kevin A. Hassett, *Dow 36,000: The New Strategy for Profiting from the Coming Rise in the Stock Market* (New York: Times Business, 1999).

8. Justin Fox, *The Myth of the Rational Market: History of Risk, Reward and Delusion on Wall Street* (New York: HarperCollins, 2009), 263.

9. Ibid.

CHAPTER 2

1. "Economic Projections and the Budget Outlook," Whitehouse.gov. Accessed March 15, 2009, at www.whitehouse.gov/administration/eop/cea/Economic-Projections-and-the-Budge-Outlook/.

2. H.15 Selected Interest Rates. Accessed March–February 2011, at www.federal reserve.gov/datadownload/Choose.aspx?rel=H.15.

3. Jon Hilsenrath, "Fed in Bond-Buying Binge to Spur Growth," *Wall Street Journal* Online, March 19, 2009: http://online.wsj.com/article/SB123739788518173569.html.

4. While earnings are released quarterly, the model was extended to monthly and daily price data by using actual closing prices for S&P 500 and 10-year Treasury yields along with S&P 500 operating earnings as a constant for each month in the quarter. The quarterly earnings were applied for the month preceding quarter-end (i.e., December–February = Q1) under the assumption that market expectations would have incorporated earning expectations. Again, it assumed that as the end of quarter approaches, earnings estimates should be reasonably close to those actual earnings ultimately reported and embodied in share prices. Earnings and S&P averages 1960 to 1987 from Damodaran Online: Home page for Answath Damodaran (New York University, http://pages.stern.nyu.edu/~adamodar/); S&P earnings and levels from 1988 to present from Standard & Poor's web site, (www.standardandpoors.com)(http://www .standardandpoors.com/indices/sp-500/en/us/?indexId=spusa-500-usduf–p-us -l–); monthly earnings for 1/86 to 11/88 from "Online Data Robert Shiller" www.econ.yale.edu/~shiller/data.htm. Calculations and methodology by the author.

5. Ibid.

6. Ibid.

7. Other standard statistical evaluations were also performed including, including examining the confidence intervals (2.5 percent – 5 percent at 95 percent confidence), plotting residuals, looking at P-values and F-test, and all yielded satisfactory results.

8. For daily calculation, actual closing prices for S&P 500 and 10-year Treasury are used; daily earnings were derived using same approach as monthly earnings as explained in Note 20.

9. Calculation of inflation expectations based on difference between 10-year Treasury yield and assumed 2 percent long-term real interest rate.

10. BBC: On This Day. "1981: Tehran Frees US Hostages after 444 Days." Accessed March 15, 2009, at http://news.bbc.co.uk/onthisday/hi/dates/stories/january/21/newsid_2506000/2506807.stm.

11. David Johnston, "Enron's Collapse: The Investigation; Justice Dept.'s Inquiry into Enron Is Beginning to Take Shape, without Big Names," *New York Times*, January 16, 2002, www.nytimes.com/2002/01/16/business/enron-s-collapse-investigation-justice-dept-s-inquiry-into-enron-beginning-take.html.

12. Elisabeth Bumiller, "Corporate Conduct: The President; Bush Signs Bill Aimed at Fraud in Corporations," *New York Times*, July 31, 2002, www.nytimes.com/2002/07/31/business/corporate-conduct-the-president-bush-signs-bill-aimed-at-fraud-in-corporations.html.

13. Alison Mitchell, "Congress Authorizes Bush to Use Force Against Iraq," *New York Times*, October 11, 2002, www.nytimes.com/2002/10/11/national/11IRAQ.html.

14. Geert Bekaert and Eric Engstrom, "Inflation and the Stock Market: Understanding the 'Fed Model,'" September 2008, www.frbsf.org/economics/conferences/0901/Bekaert-Engstrom.pdf.

15. Board of Governors of the Federal Reserve System, "Monetary Policy Report to the Congress Pursuant to the Full Employment and Balanced Growth Act of 1978," July 22, 1997, www.federalreserve.gov/boarddocs/hh/1997/july/FullReport.pdf.

16. Bekaert and Engstrom, 2008.

17. Clifford S. Asness, "Fight the Fed Model: The Relationship between Stock Market Yields, Bond Market Yields, and Future Returns," December 2002.

CHAPTER 3

1. Rajnish Mehra and Edward C. Prescott, "The Equity Premium: A Puzzle," *Journal of Monetary Economies* 15(2) (1985): 145–161.

2. Schlomo Benartzi and Richard Thaler, "Myopic Loss Aversion and the Equity Premium Puzzle," *Quarterly Journal of Economics* 110(1) (1995): 73–92.

3. Daniel Kahneman and Amos Tversky, "Prospect Theory: An Analysis of Decision under Risk," *Econometrica* 46(2) (1985): 171–185.

4. Daniel Kahneman and Amos Tversky, "Advances in Prospect Theory: Cumulative Representation of Uncertainty," *Journal of Risk and Uncertainty* 5 (1992): 297–323.

5. Daniel Kahneman, Jack L. Knetsch, and Richard H. Thaler. "The Endowment Effect, Loss Aversion, and Status Quo Bias," *Journal of Economic Perspective* 5(1) (Winter 1991): 193–206.

6. R. Thaler, A. Tversky, D. Kahneman, and A. Schwartz, "The Effect of Myopia and Loss Aversion on Risk Taking: An Experimental Test," *Quarterly Journal of Economics* 112(2) (1997).

7. Rajnish Mehra and Edward C. Prescott, "The Equity Premium in Retrospect." NBER Working Paper Series, Vol. w9525, March 2003.
8. Jonah Lehrer, *How We Decide* (New York: Houghton Mifflin Harcourt, 2009).
9. Technically, the brain stem is usually referred to as the *reptilian brain,* but the imagery of a reptile is better when thinking about these deep instinctive behaviors.
10. Benedetto De Martino, Colin F. Camerer, and Ralph Adolphs, "Amygdala Damage Eliminates Monetary Loss Aversion," *Proceedings of the National Academy of Sciences USA* (February 8, 2010), www.pnas.org/content/early/2010/02/02/0910230107.full.pdf+html.

CHAPTER 4

1. Jeffrey Nash, "Eugene Fama: The Best Advice Is 'Do Nothing,'" http://money watch.bnet.com/investing/article/eugene-fama-why-you-cant-time-the-market/277142/.
2. Fama/French Forum, "Q&A: Bias in the EMH?" www.dimensional.com/famafrench/2009/04/qa-bias-in-the-emh.html.
3. The Motley Fool, "Black Monday 10 Years Later: 1987 Timeline," March 2009, www.fool.com/features/1997/sp971017crashanniversary1987timeline.htm.
4. Source: S&P earnings and price from 1988 to present from Standard and Poor's web site (www.standardandpoors.com/indices/sp-500/en/us/?indexId=spusa-500-usduf-p-us-l-); S&P monthly earnings for 1/86 to 11/88 from "Online Data Robert Shiller" (www.econ.yale.edu/-shiller/data.htm); Treasury yields from Federal Reserve, H.15 Selected Interest Rates (www.federalreserve.gov/data download/Choose.aspx?rel=H.15). Because earnings are released quarterly, the model was extended to monthly and daily price data by using operating earnings as a constant for each month in the quarter applied for the month preceding quarter end (i.e., December to February = Q1) under the assumption that market expectations would have incorporated earning expectations. Calculations and methodology by the author.
5. John H. Cushman, Jr., "Iranian Attacks on Kuwaiti Port Called Cause for U.S. to Retaliate," *New York Times,* October 18, 1987, www.nytimes.com/1987/10/18/world/iranian-attacks-on-kuwaiti-port-called-cause-for-us-to-retaliate.html.
6. Robert J. Shiller, *Irrational Exuberance* (New York: Crown Business, 2005).
7. "S&P/Case-Shiller Home Price Indices," Standard and Poor's web site. Accessed March–April 2009, www2.standardandpoors.com/spf/pdf/index/csnational_values_022445.xls.

CHAPTER 6

1. Stephen D. Hassett, "Market Expectations for Apple, Google and Yahoo Using Real Implied Growth Rate," SeekingAlpha.com, October 14, 2010, http://seekingalpha.com/article/229979-market-expectations-for-apple-google-and-yahoo-using-real-implied-growth-rate.

2. Stephen D. Hassett, "Post-Earnings Analysis: Google Now Expected to Grow Faster than Apple," SeekingAlpha.com, October 20, 2010, http://seekingalpha.com/article/231050-post-earnings-analysis-google-now-expected-to-grow-faster-than-apple.

3. Verne G. Kopytoff and Ashlee Vance, "Sales and Profit Surge for Apple, but Its Margins Slip," *New York Times*, October 18, 2010, www.nytimes.com/2010/10/19/technology/19apple.html.

4. Dan Gallagher, "Apple's Decline in Margins Casts Shadow," MarketWatch, October 19, 2010, www.marketwatch.com/story/apple-shares-fall-on-worries-about-margins-ipad-2010-10-19.

CHAPTER 7

1. Edmund L. Andrews, "Time Warner's 'Time Machine' for Future Video," *New York Times*, December 12, 1994, www.nytimes.com/1994/12/12/business/time-warner-s-time-machine-for-future-video.html.

CHAPTER 8

1. Shannon P. Pratt and Roger J. Grabowski, *Cost of Capital: Applications and Examples* (Hoboken, NJ: John Wiley & Sons, 2010). p 36.

CHAPTER 10

1. Robert Prechter, "What Is the Elliott Wave Principle?" Retrieved December 1, 2010, from ElliotWave.com: www.elliottwave.com/introduction/elliott_wave_principle.asp.

2. Jeff Sommer, "A Market Forecast that Says 'Take Cover,'" *New York Times*, July 3, 2010, www.nytimes.com/2010/07/04/your-money/04stra.html.

3. Paul J. Lim, "A Rally that Needs More 'E.'" *New York Times*, November 28, 2009, www.nytimes.com/2009/11/29/business/economy/29fund.html?_r=2.

4. Ibid.

5. Ben Levisohn, "The Decline of the P/E Ratio," *Wall Street Journal*, August 30, 2010, http://online.wsj.com/article/SB100014240527487036185045754595 83913373278.html.

6. Ben Levisohn, "Is It Time to Scrap the Fusty Old P/E Ratio?" *Wall Street Journal*, September 4, 2010, http://online.wsj.com/article/SB1000142405274870 343160457546767186473904.html.

7. David Gaffen, "To P/E or Not to P/E? That Isn't the Appropriate Question," *Wall Street Journal*, March 3, 2009, http://online.wsj.com/article/SB12360568 8123316929.html.

8. David Leonhardt, "Remembering a Classic Investing Theory," *New York Times*, August 15, 2007, www.nytimes.com/2007/08/15/business/15leonhardt.html.

9. David Leonhardt, "Are Stocks the Bargain You Think?" *New York Times*, October 28, 2008, www.nytimes.com/2008/10/29/business/economy/29leonhardt.html.

10. Graham Bowley, "In Striking Shift, Small Investors Flee Stock Market," *New York Times*, August 21, 2010, www.nytimes.com/2010/08/22/business/22invest.html.

11. Andrea Frazzini and Owen A. Lamont, "Dumb Money: Mutual Fund Flows and the Cross-Section of Stock Returns," NBER Working Papers 11526, National Bureau of Economic Research, Inc., 2005.

12. Joan Lappin, "Bond Lemmings Headed for the Cliff," Forbes, September 7, 2010, www.forbes.com/2010/09/07/bond-bubble-dow-markets-stocks-joan-lappin.html.

13. James Altucher, "The Bears Are Dead Wrong," *WSJ Blogs*, March 16, 2010, http://blogs.wsj.com/financial-adviser/2010/03/16/the-bears-are-dead-wrong/.

About the Companion Web Site

This book includes a companion web site, which can be found at www.wiley.com/go/riskpremiumfactor (password: value123). This web site includes:

- Historical data used to construct the charts in this book, along with regular updates based on current market variables.
- Spreadsheet calculators to compute intrinsic value for the S&P 500, equity risk premium, implied growth, and implied risk-free rate.
- Links to iPhone and Android apps.
- Links to articles about the Risk Premium Factor Model.
- Contact information.

Index

Printed and bound by CPI Group (UK) Ltd, Croydon, CR0 4YY

16/04/2025

14658446-0002